The Virtual Principal

The Virtual Principal

The Many Facets of the Demanding Role

Lee A. Westberry
Tara Hornor
Mona Lise Dickson

ROWMAN & LITTLEFIELD
Lanham • Boulder • New York • London

Published by Rowman & Littlefield
An imprint of The Rowman & Littlefield Publishing Group, Inc.
4501 Forbes Boulevard, Suite 200, Lanham, Maryland 20706
www.rowman.com

86-90 Paul Street, London EC2A 4NE, United Kingdom

Copyright © 2022 by Lee A. Westberry, Tara Hornor, and Mona Lise Dickson

All rights reserved. No part of this book may be reproduced in any form or by any electronic or mechanical means, including information storage and retrieval systems, without written permission from the publisher, except by a reviewer who may quote passages in a review.

British Library Cataloguing in Publication Information Available

Library of Congress Cataloging-in-Publication Data Available
ISBN 9781475863468 (cloth) | ISBN 9781475863475 (pbk) |
 ISBN 9781475863482 (ebook)

To all educational professionals who continued fighting the good fight through the Covid-19 pandemic for the sake of our children. We humbly thank you for what you do every day!

Contents

Acknowledgments ix

Introduction xi

Chapter 1: Confidence 1

Chapter 2: Growth Mindset 15

Chapter 3: Communication and Presence 29

Chapter 4: Projecting Calm 39

Chapter 5: Technology 51

Chapter 6: Leadership Soft Skills 65

Chapter 7: Instructional Leadership 75

Chapter 8: Systems Approaches 89

Chapter 9: Challenges and Successes 109

Conclusion 121

About the Authors 123

Acknowledgments

Dr. Lee Westberry
I would like to acknowledge and express thanks to all principals who freely participated in the study. Your time is appreciated and your commitment to students is laudable. I also want to thank my family for being so supportive for the times when I am unavailable due to writing. Your patience is unwavering. I would also like to thank my oldest daughter, Warner Westberry, for being gracious enough to share her talent in providing the cover art, again.

Dr. Tara Hornor
I would like to express gratitude to the many principals who openly shared their experiences in transitioning to the virtual principalship. Their commitment and tireless efforts to influence student success were noteworthy.

My heartfelt appreciation also goes to my colleague, Dr. Lee Westberry, for the opportunity to share this research journey and explore the successes and challenges of principals during the Covid-19 pandemic. Dr. Westberry's commitment to helping enhance principal success is inspirational.

I wish to acknowledge the encouragement of my husband, Brian, dad, George, and colleagues who supported me throughout the research and writing process.

Mona Lise Dickson
I want to acknowledge my immediate and extended families, Dickson Dozen and Warrior Nation. First, my Dickson family, for your support and late nights. Then, finally, my Warrior Nation's family for investing in the systems (method of madness) for our community but especially for our students. I would also like to thank my two colleagues, Dr. Lee Westbury and Dr. Tara Hornor, for the opportunity to collaborate on Warrior Nation. Thank you both!

Introduction

In the year 2020, the world turned on its axis with the Covid-19 outbreak. In March of that year, some intercontinental travel was banned, state governments issued "stay at home" orders for all citizens, businesses closed their doors, and children were sent home from school. All of these isolating behaviors were instructed for the people's safety, as the Covid-19 virus was claiming thousands of lives and infecting millions across the world. No one was prepared, least of all schools. Imagine the task of moving over 50 million school-age students in the United States alone to a virtual environment overnight!

The impact on teachers and student learning is being studied at a rapid pace, for many fear the learning gaps that are being produced due to the pandemic. However, very little is discussed about the impact of the Covid-19 pandemic on the principal. Today's principalship is difficult enough with the changing demands and increased accountability. Add to that the drastic and rapid change to virtual leadership versus traditional leadership, and the impact is larger than many imagine. Through the course of surveys and interviews, the "gem" of a virtual principal was discovered.

When examining and evaluating virtual administrative practices, the comparison can be made to the evaluation of a diamond. How is a diamond evaluated? A diamond is characterized by the four C's: carat, color, clarity, and cut. When mining for an effective virtual principal, these four characteristics were relevant. Let's map those out in comparison to the factors of the virtual principalship in Table I.1 below. This book will address all four characteristics of an effective virtual principal and provide insight into how states and districts can support their administrators in this unprecedented time. Hopefully, US schools will not have to face a similar occurrence; however, the virtual aspect of schooling has opened new doors, and districts and administrators need to be prepared. The role of the principal is too important to ignore the "gem" of a virtual principal.

Throughout this book, case study samples and vignettes are provided from a principal's perspective in the form of *Principal's Corners*. This principal successfully maneuvered the pandemic through her virtual leadership, and her experiences are shared in the hopes that others can relate and pick up some tidbits of knowledge. This South Carolina leader has led her high minority, high poverty school to high levels of achievement as her school has been awarded with the Gene Bottom's Pacesetter Award.

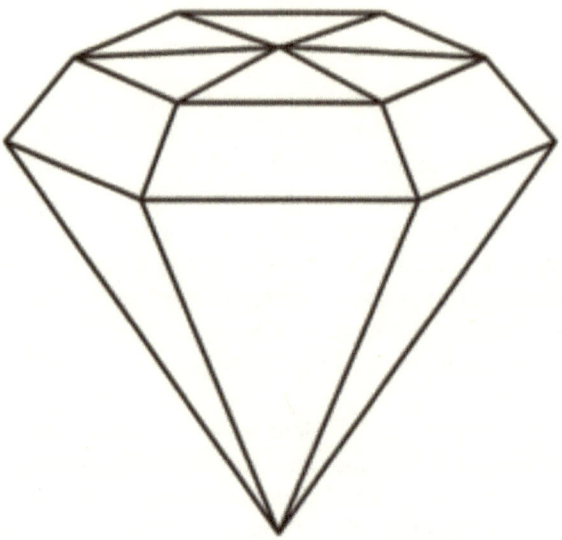

Table I.1: Four factors to evaluate a diamond in comparison to the virtual principalship.

Carat	Color	Clarity	Cut
The carat is weight of the diamond—the weight of the impact of Covid-19 on principals—confidence and growth.	The visible color of the stone can be compared to the visible factors in the principalship—communication, soft skills, etc.	The clearer, the more brilliant the stone—the more value. Instructional leadership and systems approaches make expectations clear.	The cut of the stone is determined by its depth and angles. These factors affect how light shines through the stone. Examining successes and challenges is akin to the cut.

Chapter 1

Confidence

As long as you keep going, you'll keep getting better. And as you get better, you gain more confidence. That alone is success.

—Tamara Taylor

THE PANDEMIC

The Covid-19 pandemic wreaked havoc on the national health-care system with overrun hospitals and a shortage of staff, and it created a downturn in the economy with businesses closing and people out of work. Additionally, the virus created chaos amidst workplace settings with the Center for Disease Control and Prevention's guidelines (essential workplaces, social distancing, and protective equipment) as a result of the spread of the virus. As of March 6, 2021, over 28 million cases of the coronavirus were confirmed in the United States, and over 520,000 deaths have occurred due to this deadly virus (Centers for Disease Control and Prevention, 2021).

Educational settings have not been immune to the effects of Covid-19. In fact, schools closed and delayed openings across the world as a way to curb the spread of the virus (Kim et al., 2020; Stage et al., 2020). For the spring of 2020, "close to 80 percent of the world's student population [war] affected by school closures in 138 countries" (Chang & Yano, 2020, p. 1). Furthermore, many schools, both K–12 and higher education, across the world have turned toward some form of virtual instruction for students in order to inhibit the infection rates (Black, Ferdig, & Thompson, 202).

This virtual learning has taken many shapes and forms. For example, some school districts chose to move instruction fully online with no children or teachers in the school buildings. Other districts have utilized a hybrid approach where groups of students alternate days to attend school, thereby reducing the number of students in attendance on any given day by half. Still, other districts created a virtual academy for students who chose to attend, while the remaining students attended school face-to-face five days a week. Furthermore, some districts had teachers teaching students face-to-face and in the virtual environment simultaneously. Each approach brought new challenges and problems for students, teachers, and administrators.

With the need for an online learning platform in virtual schooling, school leaders were faced with many new questions to answer. What is the status of digital learning currently in our school? What percentage of students have internet access and devices? What happens with the students who do not have access? What digital platform will be used for learning? How will teachers receive training on the platform to not only teach, grade, but also engage students virtually? These are only a few questions that have been faced by school leaders during this pandemic (Schleicher, 2020). Certainly, Covid-19 created problems that needed to be solved rapidly for the sake of student learning.

THE STUDY

In a recent mixed-method research study conducted in a southern state, principals were asked about their experiences as a virtual principal since the Covid-19 pandemic began. Superintendents were also asked about their perceptions of their principals' needs during the pandemic. This study included surveys of seventy-seven principals and superintendents as well as ten structured interviews with both principals and superintendents.

Principals and superintendents who participated in the qualitative component of this study answered a variety of interview questions designed to generate insight into the following questions: How do principals and superintendents describe the knowledge, skills, and abilities necessary for being an effective virtual principal? How did the transition to virtual education impact principals? All of the participants interviewed in this research study reported the knowledge, skills, and abilities required by a virtual principalship role differed from those required by traditional principalship roles.

The survey was based on the multiple roles that principals must perform simultaneously, from a manager of resources to an instructional leader to an administrator who deals with day-to-day operations of schools (Hallinger, 2010; Kowalski, 2010; Naidoo, 2019). Hallinger (2011) began the study of the three-prong system of the principalship and noted the three main avenues through which leadership is believed to be linked to learning: vision and goals, academic structures and processes, and people. However, this study applied these three prongs to the virtual world.

Vision and goals provide the school and the community the aspirations for the school and how that direction will be achieved: program administration.

The academic structures and processes include the curriculum, teaching, and learning, which is instructional leadership, the basis for school improvement. Management skills are needed to handle personnel, students, and parents. How did principal performance fare in the virtual world? How did principals handle the abrupt transition?

Hanna, an experienced high school principal, elaborated on her transition to virtual leadership:

> This is year nine for me in this seat and after a while you get to a point where you feel like you've seen pretty much everything and how to handle everything. And what it did was it basically took me down to being a first-year principal again in some cases. I'll be honest in saying that unlike first-year principals who you know are first-year principals and people are giving them support, I think we all felt like first-year principals again in so many cases. No one knew how to support us because they were flying by seat of their pants too in terms of what is needed.

In fact, the majority of principals participating in the study used the term "flying by the seat of our pants" when describing the transition to the virtual principalship. This sentiment led the discussion to confidence, or self-efficacy.

Self-Efficacy

Albert Bandura (1997) theorized in his social cognitive theory (SCT) that the way people feel about their capabilities and the outcomes of their efforts will influence the way people behave. Three major assumptions exist with SCT:

1. People can learn through observation, even if they have had no prior experience.
2. Reinforcement is key to learning, but it is not all external. Intrinsic motivation is key to the mental preparedness to learn.
3. Changed behaviors do not necessarily result from something that has been learned. Self-regulation is necessary in order for change to happen and be sustained (Bandura, 1991).

As Bandura (1991) points out, mental preparedness for learning is also key. Principals did not have the luxury of mental preparedness during the pandemic because the decision was made to close schools abruptly. This quick decision led to many problems that had to be solved just as quickly. Problem solving, according to Payne and Wenger (1998), includes two elements:

1. a description of all possible states of the task and problem solver (representation), and
2. a list of the ways of moving among those states (search). The first element supports a problem solver to understand the problem by abstraction and identification. The second element enables the problem solver to search for a possible solution in memory (p. 82)

For principals to be effective in solving the problems caused by the pandemic, they must first fully understand the problems and all possible solutions. Again, principals could not preplan to problem solve due to the unexpected nature and timeframe of the schools closing. In addition, many of these solutions are not within a principal's control due to lack of autonomy (Dou, Devos, & Valcke, 2017; Paufler, 2018). Districts were making decisions quickly, and these decisions impacted all schools within that district.

Furthermore, principals most likely have never faced anything similar to the pandemic experience, so they do not have memory-based solutions to draw upon. Finally, principals may have experienced increased stress and anxiety due to the pandemic and the impact on their own families and communities (Canet-Juric et al., 2020; Montemurro, 2020; Pedrosa et al., 2020). One must remember that principals are family members before they are principals.

In the context of the Covid-19 pandemic, principals have not had the opportunity to observe virtual leadership much less understand it fully, and this led to struggles. The pandemic's timeline thrust schools into action without the time for planning, preparation, and procurement of resources—basic tenets of quality professional development (Guskey, 2003; Guskey & Yoon, 2009). Hence, the "flying by the seat of my pants" comment was a common thread in interviews. Jack, a first-year principal, shared the following observation:

The transition was frightening. I'm the only high school in my district so I don't have other high school principals within my district to bounce ideas off of. . . . I do have other principals throughout the state and throughout the country that I could call but their circumstances are totally different than my circumstances. They might have a plethora of resources to pull from whereas I might not. So I'm having to be innovative in some of the decisions that I make.

Consequently, Bandura (2006) expanded his SCT theory to include the important element of self-efficacy, the belief in one's own ability to be successful in task completion and dealing with stressors. Self-efficacy has been studied at length in education, to include the impact on student achievement (Soehner & Ryan, 2011; Terziu, Hasani ,& Osmani, 2016), the impact on teacher effectiveness (Fiaz et al., 2017; Francis, 2017; Ma & Marion, 2019), and the impact on principal satisfaction (Baroudi & Hojeij, 2018; Gulmez & Negis Isik, 2020).

However, self-efficacy in the face of a pandemic may not equate to that of a traditional setting. Recent research has shown that self-efficacy is lower related to Covid-19 (Yıldırım & Guler, 2020), which directly impacts how people act regarding risk-taking behaviors (Wong & Yang, 2020). Risk-taking behaviors are deemed positive since that is how professionals learn and grow. This negative impact affects teachers and students, which in turn, directly impacts principals.

When asked how the transition to the virtual environment influenced her confidence, Donna, a high school principal with three years of experience, chuckled and stated the following: "On a scale of one to ten, ten being confident, any day walking into my building I feel I'm at a nine. With virtual, I'd put myself at a three maybe a four." If principals are feeling insecure, the trickle-down effect has to impact the rest of the staff who are also experiencing new challenges and difficulties. Most interview participants also characterized the virtual principalship as "more challenging," "more difficult," "harder," and more "time intensive" than leading in traditional face-to-face educational environments.

COLLECTIVE SELF-EFFICACY

Principals with a strong self-efficacy are more likely to persevere through the challenges faced in schools and positively impact teacher self-efficacy (Li & Liu, 2020; Liu & Hallinger, 2018; Sehgal, Nambudiri, & Mishra, 2017). In fact, a principal's self-efficacy has a positive correlation to the collective self-efficacy of a school (Hosseingholizadeh, Amrahi, & El-Farr, 2020; Supriadi & Suryana, 2021).

This collective self-efficacy is the confidence that both the individuals (teacher, student, and principal) and the collective whole will be able to carry out the behaviors of teaching and learning (Bandura, 1997). These self-confident beliefs have shown to be predictive of academic behaviors (Bandura, 1997). See Figure 1.1 for an illustration of collective self-efficacy.

In consequence to the pandemic, societal norms (isolation and social distancing) as well as individual beliefs (individual health and safety) have changed; the question remains if the collective self-efficacy that once existed in schools still remains. In essence, did the pandemic have a negative impact on a school's collective self-efficacy? The hard truth is that teachers experienced lower self-efficacy in using technology with a lack of support and resources to teach online. In addition, teachers have experienced difficulty motivating students in the online environment (Cardullo et al., 2021).

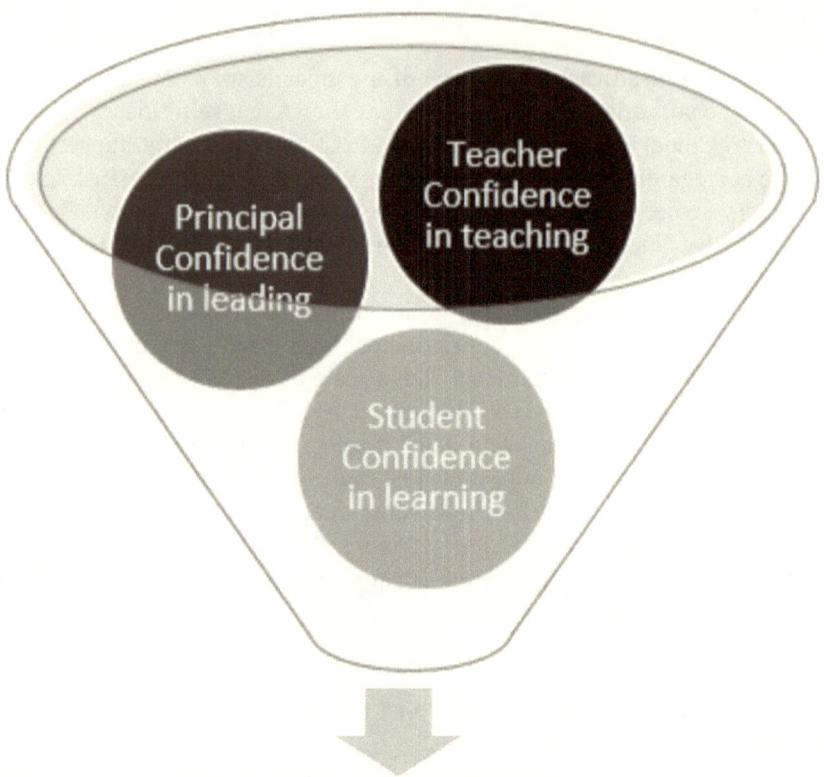

Figure 1.1 Collective self-efficacy

Administrators are charged with growing leadership capacity in their buildings (Brown, 2015; Stringer & Hourani, 2016), which has a direct correlation with teacher confidence (Liu, Bellibaş, & Gümüş, 2020; Li & Liu, 2018; Ozdemir, Sahin, & ztürkOzturk, 2020). However, the pandemic's impact on teachers may not leave room for more responsibilities and additional capacity building because teachers, themselves, are struggling. Teachers are charged with providing quality instruction as well as student accountability in the virtual setting. Korman, O'Keefe, and Repka (2020) have noted, "For approximately 3 million of the most educationally marginalized students in the country, March [2020] might have been the last time they experienced any formal education—virtual or otherwise" (para. 1). Many students have not been participating in their education, and teachers are accountable for student achievement. This contradictory condition has left many schools scrambling to address the learning losses, which puts even more pressure on administrators and teachers.

For example, the learning gaps that are anticipated to exist at the beginning of the 2021 school year span from six months' to a year's worth of learning, depending on the ethnicity and socioeconomic status of students (Dorn et al., 2020). Couple the stress of addressing the gaps with the changing societal norms and individual beliefs during the pandemic, and teachers might already be beyond capacity.

UNINTENDED CONSEQUENCES

Change

Despite the challenges faced and impact of the self-efficacy of principals as well as the collective self-efficacy of a school, the rapid switch to the virtual setting did have some positive, unintended consequences. One upshot of the pandemic is that change, which is so hard for many, has become a necessity. Newton and Tarrant (1992) state that change "can be stressful and can easily lack proper personnel support for the people involved. Feelings are regularly hurt, and some individuals sustain long-term damage through efforts toward short-term change. Change can be both exhilarating and painful" (p. 1). This forced change has impacted the organizational culture of many schools.

Organizational culture "refers to a set of common values, attitudes, beliefs and norms, some of which are explicit and some of which are not" (Brown, 2004, p. 4). This culture can be found in the nature of relationships, school norms, and shared experiences (Haberman, 2013). This change in culture, of course, can be positive or negative; however, the pandemic forced a change nonetheless, and this study found a positive change.

Melanie, a high school principal with over ten years of experience, shared that the created a supportive condition in her school, stating they have "grown even stronger as a family, working together. We are all in this together—to make it work it's going to take us all."

Likewise, Christina, an experienced superintendent stated that the pandemic "strengthened our team."

Hanna, an experienced high school principal, stated, "I fought change. . . . I have always [believed] kids need to be in school, they need to be in front of teachers. . . . I guess I wish I wouldn't have been so stubborn."

Donna, a high school principal with three years' experience, shared, "I do feel we are better prepared if we do need to shut down . . . whether it's a pandemic, a hurricane, or an ice storm."

In essence, Covid-19 forced schools to change, and this change was positive for many. The process of change is hard because people are often motivated by negatives such as fear, which can lead to stress and resistance; however, this fear is often rooted in fear of failure (Calarco, 2020). If a staff feels supported throughout a process, then the fear subsides. One has to remember that change is a process, and it does not take place overnight. See Figure 1.2 for an illustration of the impact of change with and without supports.

Social/Emotional Aspects

Even though the required change has been good for some schools, the social and emotional toll on principals has been markedly higher than pre-Covid times. Social-emotional learning (SEL) has earned a spotlight in today's classrooms due to the number of difficulties children face today: poverty, home life, homelessness, bullying, cyber bullying, and so on. In fact, suicide was the second leading cause of death in people aged ten to fourteen, fifteen to twenty-four, and twenty-five to thirty-four in 2018 (2021). Because children face more obstacles today than ever before, schools have endeavored to include SEL in the classrooms.

SEL includes the following:

- Maintaining cooperative relationships
- Making responsible decisions
- Managing strong emotions
- Solving problems effectively
- Recognizing emotions in oneself and others
- Having empathy for others (Is & Matters, 2019, p. 1).

Now, apply this to the principal's position during this pandemic. Principals have been faced with making responsible decisions, maintaining cooperative relationships virtually, solving problems effectively, and recognizing the

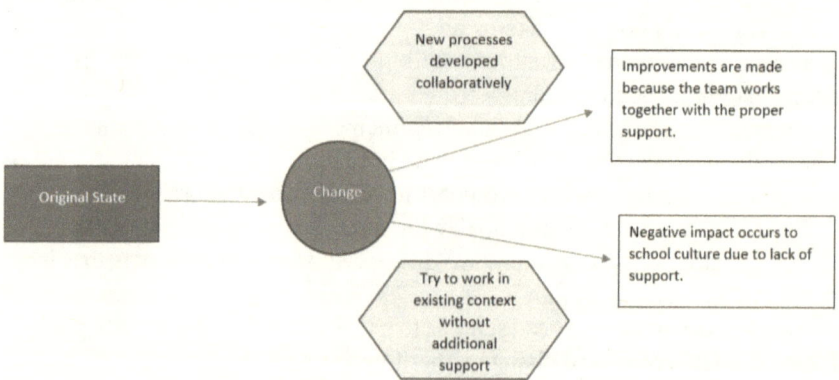

Figure 1.2 Impact of change pathways

emotions of others and giving them validity, among other tasks. Even though principals manage these tasks in a normal setting, add to that the increased challenges of the abrupt virtual setting, and the social/emotional toll has been difficult to manage.

When asked about her transition to virtual leadership, Hanna, an experienced high school principal, reported it made her feel "angry and alone. You feel alone sometimes in this position . . . and I felt like I couldn't share [those feelings]." Hannah continued to use terms such as "weary," "exhausted," and "felt stupid." Jack, a first-year high school principal, described the virtual principalship as "a lonely seat." Finally, Don, an experienced superintendent, shared that "the fear, the worry, the concern is real."

The need for principal assistance during this time should be the impetus for district leaders to provide social and emotional support. "Support," by its very definition, means to provide a foundation and/or assistance. Understanding support structures that provide sustainable aid and opportunities for growth are critical, as the principal has a direct impact on teacher effectiveness and student achievement (Ma & Marion, 2019; Naidoo, 2019).

Mentoring is noted to increase self-confidence and encourage risk-taking behaviors, but in order for mentoring to work, the organizational culture must exist to support mentoring. For example, a district must support the open communication free of evaluation as well as provide the time for proper mentoring to exist (Ragins & Kram, 2007). Additionally, these mentors would need to be trained on how to provide the proper support and not just allow a check-in system.

Coaching is another viable option for principal support. Schools employ myriad coaches: instructional, technology, literacy, and so on. All of these coaches work one-on-one with teachers. Principals deserve the same kind of support, particularly in the form of leadership coaching. What better time to provide quality coaching? Research suggests that coaches from within the organization have a greater impact (Hong & Rainey, 2019; Jones, Woods, & Guillaume, 2016), and district leaders could surely fill this void.

Communities of practice, or CoP, are "groups of people who share a concern or passion for something they do and learn how to do it better as they interact regularly" (Wenger, 2011, p. 1). This is an optimal support for continued learning. If principals were given the time to work together to problem solve the issues they are facing, then this CoP could provide a great support to alleviate the emotional toll the pandemic is taking. See Table 1.1 for a chart of the types of supports for principals that can work to alleviate the social/emotional toll of the pandemic and help build confidence.

Table 1.1: Types of Support for Principals

Mentoring	Coaching	Communities of Practice
One-to-One Support Mentor provides guidance and advice.	One-to-One Coach works to develop job-related skills through the process of feedback.	Small Group Mutual engagement of CoP members to share best practices and solve common problems.

SUMMARY

During the Covid-19 pandemic, principals found themselves "flying by the seat of their pants." In other words, they were not prepared for what faced them as they were plunged into the virtual principalship. As a result of the abrupt change, principal self-efficacy was impacted greatly. Self-efficacy is the belief in oneself and one's abilities. The SCT of self-efficacy is rooted in three major factors: learning through observation, mental preparedness to learn, and self-regulation. Most principals were not equipped for the transition to virtual schooling as they were not prepared and had not observed the virtual principalship before.

The collective self-efficacy of schools was also negatively impacted. Collective self-efficacy is the belief that the collective whole (principal, teacher, and student) can achieve its shared goal—academic learning. Teachers, students, and principals experienced a negative hit to their self-efficacy.

A couple of unintended consequences did surface during the transition to the virtual principalship. One unintended consequence is the culture of change. Many schools experienced the organizational culture of the school to adopt the culture of change, which became a positive consequence.

A second unintended consequence is the social/emotional toll that principals have experienced. Districts should provide support for principals in one or more of the following ways: mentoring, coaching, and/or communities of practice.

POLISHING THE DIAMOND

1. How did principals fare with the transition to the virtual principalship? Give examples.
2. What is self-efficacy?
3. Explain how principals' self-efficacy was impacted by the Covid-19 pandemic and why.
4. What is collective self-efficacy?

5. Explain how a school's collective self-efficacy was impacted by the Covid-19 pandemic and why.
6. What are two unintended consequences of the transition to the virtual principalship?
7. How can districts support principals in the social/emotional domain? List three ways.

REFERENCES

Bandura, A. (1991). Social cognitive theory of self-regulation. *Organizational Behavior and Human Decision Processes, 50*(2), 248–287.

Bandura, A. (1997). Self-efficacy: The exercise of control. New York: Freeman Press.

Bandura, A. (2006). Guide for constructing self-efficacy scales. In F. Pajares & T. Urdan (Eds.), *Self-efficacy beliefs of adolescents* (Vol. 5, pp. 307–337). Greenwich, CT: Information Age Publishing.

Baroudi, S., & Hojeij, Z. (2018). The role of self-efficacy as an attribute of principals' leadership effectiveness in K–12 private and public institutions in Lebanon. *International Journal of Leadership in Education, 23*(4), 457–471.

Black, E., Ferdig, R., & Thompson, L. A. (2021). K–12 virtual schooling, COVID-19, and student success. *JAMA Pediatrics, 175*(2), 119–120. doi: 10.1001/jamapediatrics.2020.3800

Brown, G., III. (2015). What's the difference? Principal practices that support the achievement of low-income students in demographically diverse schools. *Academy of Educational Leadership Journal, 19*(2), 11–31.

Brown, R. (2004). *School culture and organization: Lessons from research and experience* [A background paper for the Denver Commission on Secondary School Reform]. https://www.dpsk12.org/pdf/culture_organization.pdf

Calarco, A. (2020). *Adaptable leadership: What it takes to be a quick change artist.* White paper from the Center for Creative Leadership. https://files.eric.ed.gov/fulltext/ED606779.pdf

Canet-Juric, L., Andrés, M. L., Del Valle, M., López-Morales, H., Poó, F., Galli, J. I., & Urquijo, S. (2020). A longitudinal study on the emotional impact caused by the COVID-19 pandemic quarantine on general population. *Frontiers in Psychology, 11*, 2431.

Cardullo, V., Wang, C., Burton, M., & Dong, J. (2021). K–12 teachers' remote teaching self-efficacy during the pandemic. *Journal of Research in Innovative Teaching & Learning*, ahead of print. https://doi.org/10.1108/JRIT-10-2020-0055

Centers for Disease Control and Prevention (2021). Covid tracker data. https://covid.cdc.gov/covid-data-tracker/#cases_casesper100klast7days

Chang, G. C., & Yano, S. (2020). *How are countries addressing the Covid-19 challenges in education? A snapshot of policy measures.* UNESCO.

Dorn, E., Hancock, B., Sarakatsannis, J., & Viruleg, E. (2020). *COVID-19 and learning loss—Disparities grow and students need help.* McKinsey & Company.

https://www.mckinsey.com/industries/public-and-social-sector/our-insights/covid-19-and-learning-loss-disparities-grow-and-students-need-help

Dou, D., Devos, G., & Valcke, M. (2017). The relationships between school autonomy gap, principal leadership, teachers' job satisfaction and organizational commitment. *Educational Management Administration & Leadership, 45*(6), 959–977.

Fiaz, M., Qin, S., Ikram, A., & Saqib, A. (2017). Leadership styles and employees' motivation: Perspective from an emerging economy. *Journal of Developing Areas, 51*(4), 143–156.

Francis, C. U. (2017). Transformational and transactional leadership styles among leaders of administrative ministries in Lagos, Nigeria. *IFE Psychologia: An International Journal*, (2), 151–164.

Gulmez, D., & Negis Isik, A. (2020). The correlation between school principals' self-efficacy beliefs and leadership styles. *International Online Journal of Educational Sciences, 12*(1), 326–327.

Guskey, T. R. (2003). What makes professional development effective? *Phi Delta Kappan, 84*(10), 748–750.

Guskey, T. R., & Yoon, K. S. (2009). What works in professional development? *Phi Delta Kappan, 90*(7), 495–500.

Haberman, M. (2013). Why school culture matters, and how to improve it. *Huffington Post*. http://www.huffingtonpost.com/Michael-Haberman/why-school-culture-matter_b_3047318.html

Hallinger, P. (2010). Developing instructional leadership. In B. Davies & M. Brundrett (Eds)., *Developing successful leadership: Studies in educational leadership, 11*. New York: Springer.

Hallinger, P. (2011). Leadership for learning: Lessons from 40 years of empirical research. *Journal of Educational Administration, 49*(2), 125–142.

Hong, M., & Rainey, L. (2019). Supporting principal supervisors: What really matters? *Journal of Educational Administration, 57*(5), 455–462.

Hosseingholizadeh, R., Amrahi, A., & El-Farr, H. (2020). Instructional leadership, and teacher's collective efficacy, commitment, and professional learning in primary schools: A mediation model. *Professional Development in Education*, 1–18.

Is, W. I., & Matters, W. I. (2019). Social-emotional learning. *USA: Committee for Children*. https://www.cfchildren.org/wp-content/uploads/policy-advocacy/what-and-why-one-pager.pdf

Jones, R., Woods, S., & Guillaume, Y. (2016). The effectiveness of workplace coaching: A meta-analysis of learning and performance outcomes from coaching. *Journal of Occupational and Organizational Psychology, 89*, 249–277.

Kim, S., Kim, Y. J., Peck, K. R., & Jung, E. (2020). School opening delay effect on transmission dynamics of coronavirus disease 2019 in Korea: Based on mathematical modeling and simulation study. *Journal of Korean Medical Science, 35*(13).

Korman, H., O'Keefe, B., & Repka, M. (2020). Missing in the margins: Estimating the scale of the COVID-19 attendance crisis. *Missing in the Margins: Estimating the Scale of the COVID-19 Attendance Crisis*. Bellwether Education Partners

Kowalski, T. (2010). *The school principal: Visionary leadership and competent management*. New York: Routledge.

Li, L., & Liu, Y. (2020). An integrated model of principal transformational leadership and teacher leadership that is related to teacher self-efficacy and student academic performance. *Asia Pacific Journal of Education*, 1–18.

Liu, S., & Hallinger, P. (2018). Principal instructional leadership, teacher self-efficacy, and teacher professional learning in China: Testing a mediated-effects model. *Educational Administration Quarterly, 54*(4), 501–528.

Liu, Y., Bellibaş, M. Ş., & Gümüş, S. (2020). The effect of instructional leadership and distributed leadership on teacher self-efficacy and job satisfaction: Mediating roles of supportive school culture and teacher collaboration. *Educational Management Administration & Leadership*, 1–24,

Ma, X., & Marion, R. (2019). Exploring how instructional leadership affects teacher efficacy: A multilevel analysis. *Educational Management Administration & Leadership*. https://doi.org/10.1177/1741143219888742

Molden, D. C., & Dweck, C. S. (2006). Finding "meaning" in psychology: A lay theories approach to self-regulation, social perception, and social development. *American Psychologist, 61*(3), 192.

Montemurro, N. (2020). The emotional impact of COVID-19: From medical staff to common people. *Brain, Behavior, and Immunity*. doi: 10.1016/j.bbi.2020.03.032

Naidoo, P. (2019). Perceptions of teachers and school management teams of the leadership roles of public school principals. *South African Journal of Education, 39*(2), 1–14.

National Institute of Mental Health (2021). Suicide is a leading cause of death in the United States. https://www.nimh.nih.gov/health/statistics/suicide.shtml

Newton, C., & Tarrant, T., (1992). *Managing change in schools: A practical handbook*. New York: Routledge.

Özdemir, G., Sahin, S., & Öztürk, N. (2020). Teachers' self-efficacy perceptions in terms of school principal's instructional leadership behaviours. *International Journal of Progressive Education, 16*(1), 25–40.

Paufler, N. A. (2018). Declining morale, diminishing autonomy, and decreasing value: Principal reflections on a high-Stakes teacher evaluation system. *International Journal of Education Policy and Leadership, 13*(8).

Payne, D. G., & Wenger, M. J. (1998). *Cognitive psychology*. Boston: Houghton Mifflin Company

Pedrosa, A. L., Bitencourt, L., Fróes, A. C. F., Cazumbá, M. L. B., Campos, R. G. B., de Brito, S. B. C. S., & e Silva, A. C. S. (2020). Emotional, behavioral, and psychological impact of the COVID-19 pandemic. *Frontiers in Psychology, 11*.

Ragins, B. R., & Kram, K. (2007). *The handbook of mentoring at work: Theory, research, and practice*. Los Angeles: SAGE.

Schleicher, A. (2020). *The impact of Covid-19 on education: Insights from Education at a Glance 2020*. OECD.

Sehgal, P., Nambudiri, R., & Mishra, S. K. (2017). Teacher effectiveness through self-efficacy, collaboration and principal leadership. *International Journal of Educational Management, 34*(4), 505–517.

Soehner, D., & Ryan, T. (2011). The interdependence of principal school leadership and student achievement. *Scholar-Practitioner, 5*(3), 274–288.

Stage, H. B., Shingleton, J., Ghosh, S., Scarabel, F., Pellis, L., & Finnie, T. (2020). Shut and re-open: The role of schools in the spread of COVID-19 in Europe. *Philosophical Transactions of the Royal Society B: Biological Sciences.* doi: 10.1098/rstb.2020.0277

Stringer, P., & Hourani, R. B. (2016). Transformation of roles and responsibilities of principals in times of change. *Educational Management Administration & Leadership, 44*(2), 224–246.

Supriadi, A. C., & Suryana, A. (2021, February). Impact of leadership efficacy on teacher teaching performance in elementary schools. In *4th International Conference on Research of Educational Administration and Management (ICREAM 2020)* (115–118). Atlantis Press.

Terziu, L., Hasani, N., & Osmani, O. (2016). The role of the school principal in increasing students' success. *Revista de Stinte Politice, 50,* 103–113.

Wenger, E. (2011). *Communities of practice: A brief introduction.* National Science Foundation.

Wong, J. C. S., & Yang, J. Z. (2020). Seeing is believing: Examining self-efficacy and trait hope as moderators of youths' positive risk-taking intention. *Journal of Risk Research,* 1–14.

Yeager, D. S., & Dweck, C. S. (2012). Mindsets that promote resilience: When students believe that personal characteristics can be developed. *Educational Psychologist, 47*(4), 302–314.

Yıldırım, M., & Guler, A. (2020). Factor analysis of the COVID-19 perceived risk scale: A preliminary study. *Death Studies.* doi: 10.1080/07481187.2020.1784311

Chapter 2

Growth Mindset

Life keeps throwing me stones. And I keep finding the diamonds.

—Ana Claudia Antunes

NAVIGATING CHALLENGES

The pandemic and the transition to virtual principalship presented countless challenges to navigate throughout K–12 learning environments. Many principals found themselves navigating challenges they never desired or even imagined having to overcome in their professional careers, including figuring out how to transition an entire learning organization to virtual instruction, leading a virtual workforce, and overseeing sanitation and disease prevention processes during a worldwide pandemic.

The difficulties of navigating these challenges were further compounded by having to lead and project calm during a time of great uncertainty, fear, and health risk. Adding to the complexity of the leadership challenge, virtual principals also found themselves navigating obstacles in technology and communication processes, as well as establishing food distribution and virtual counseling processes to meet students' basic needs.

REQUIRED KNOWLEDGE, SKILLS, AND ABILITIES

Principals participating in the study universally described the virtual principalship as a challenge, necessitating the acquisition of distinct knowledge, skills, and abilities in several key areas. Interview participants identified five distinct areas of knowledge, skills, and abilities as central to being an effective virtual principal: (1) ability to demonstrate a strong sense of presence and sustain frequent communications, (2) capability to project calm during uncertainty, (3) skill in conveying flexibility, empathy, and patience, (4) strong knowledge of technology capabilities, and (5) proficiency in the utilization of a systems approach to sustain strong instructional leadership practices.

The need to learn these new skills associated with virtual principalship presented a significant challenge to overcome. In the mixed-method study, over 96 percent of principals rated their confidence as "high" or "very high" in traditional instructional settings, while less than half that amount, only 40.9 percent, reported a "high" or "very high" confidence level in virtual settings. The differential in the percentage of principals reporting "very high" confidence levels when leading in traditional environments (72.7 percent of respondents) and virtual principalship (only 9.7 percent of respondents) was noteworthy.

The difference was eye-opening. Principals were far more likely to rate their confidence level as a virtual principal as "moderate" (51.9 percent of respondents), whereas only 2.6 percent of principals rated their confidence level as "moderate" in traditional instructional settings. Maybe principals having to leave their comfort zones contributed to the decline in confidence.

Notably, principals approached this challenge with different attitudes, perspectives, and strategies. However, those who successfully transitioned to the virtual principalship role demonstrated one key characteristic, a growth mindset. They believed they could learn and develop the knowledge, skills, and abilities required to be an effective virtual principal to meet the needs of their students, teachers, staff, and communities.

TRANSITION TO GROWTH MINDSET

The transition to the virtual principalship required an openness to new opportunities and ways of operating. Principals needed to navigate these challenges with a growth mindset. Carol Dweck's (2006) book, *Mindset: The Psychology of Success*, presents the concepts of two dueling ways of conceptualizing and navigating challenges. Dweck (2006) asserts that individuals view challenge with either a fixed mindset or a growth mindset. In a fixed mindset, leaders view their knowledge, skills, and abilities in a static or fixed way,

> *Growth mindset is based on the belief that your basic qualities are things you can cultivate through your efforts, your strategies, and help from others.*
>
> —Carol Dweck

Principals play a critical leadership role in helping their learning organizations navigate change. The shift to virtual instruction prompted principals to reflect on how they would navigate new challenges. Principals essentially had to ask themselves, How do I lead the organization virtually? Will I avoid challenge and potential failure? Or will I view the new circumstances as an opportunity?

How leaders viewed their own "talents and abilities" mattered. Leaders' attitudes and perceptions about their own abilities guide how they perceive and approach challenges as well as how they model a growth mindset to others. In essence, growth spurs growth, and confidence bestows confidence.

In the mixed-method research study, each of the interview participants expressed the transition to virtual principalship offered several silver linings and unexpected areas of personal and organizational growth. Interview participants identified three distinct areas where a growth mindset emerged as a result of the transition to virtual principalship, including increased self-efficacy and confidence, growth in instructional leadership skills, and enhanced team cohesion.

Growth Mindset Led to Increased Confidence

During the individual interviews, all ten principals and superintendents expressed self-efficacy and confidence gains resulting from the transition to the virtual principalship, as opposed to where they rated themselves at the beginning of the pandemic. Hanna, an experienced high school principal, also shared, "I've had to become really a lot more savvy." Similarly, Jack, a first-year principal, shared, "I think I'm an expert now. I can go anywhere and get any job. . . . I've grown leaps and bounds."

John, a high school principal with four years of experience, stated,

> The confidence factor is huge and feeling like I'm supported by my district is huge as well. So I've got confidence in what I do on a daily basis now. I'm confident I have confidence from my district because I've produced gains in the years that I've been here that [have] induced that confidence, but it allowed me to be focused on what I think is probably the most critical aspect of leadership during this time, which is keeping the morale and the mindset of teachers checked in. So I say one thing we've done successfully is we've had a tremendous focus on supporting our teachers.

Seaton's (2018) research suggests that leaders' growth mindsets can influence the mindsets of teachers and students as well as their levels of confidence. The trickle-down effect is real. Principals with growth mindsets have a powerful opportunity to model a commitment to continuous learning and improvement to the entire learning community.

Growth Mindset Led to Stronger Instructional Leadership Skills

Growth in instructional leadership skills and experiences was a second critical finding identified by the overwhelming majority of interview participants. Hanna, an experienced high school principal, stated,

> It was an "aha" moment for me when I realized when I was popping into these classrooms and I'm having these conversations with teachers how much I really didn't know what was going on in my building, even though I thought I did, even though I thought I had a good handle on it. That's when you see your weaknesses.

Likewise, Melanie, an experienced high school principal, commented,

> You gotta look at the details of everything. And I think even as a brick-and-mortar leader, I paid attention to those little things, but now I'm even paying attention closer to not only what I do, how I do it, but I'm paying attention to my people and my leadership team as well, to make sure that we are communicating.

Jack, a first-year principal, shared how the transition had helped him "refine data collection and disseminating that data." Kay, an experienced high school principal, noted the transition helped her in "learning how to manipulate technology for best practices." In addition, Donna, a principal with three years of experience, noted the transition had caused her to be "much more engaged with students and curriculum." Christina, an experienced superintendent, shared,

> I think that we are, we're more deliberate. We're more thoughtful. . . . We're more thoughtful of the needs of our teachers. . . . What type of professional development do they need? What type of learning experiences do they need?

Each of these principals' instructional leadership skills were strengthened because they took the step to learn or try something new. They approached the changes the pandemic caused in their own lives and workplaces with a growth mindset. For example, Hanna's new approach of popping into classrooms to talk with teachers expanded her understanding of the learning community and provided a new avenue to gain information and other perspectives in the future. Kay's growth mindset during the pandemic led her to learn more about technology best practices that could aid her school. These "aha moments" and instructional leadership skill gains will likely persist far beyond the pandemic.

Growth Mindset Led to Enhanced Team Cohesion

All of the interview participants expressed that working through the challenges associated with transitioning to virtual instruction led to enhanced team cohesion. This sentiment is described by Jack, a first-year principal, who shared,

> I'm surrounded by a lot of hardworking, dedicated people who understand the struggles of this community and want to see change and want to see our progress and move in the right direction.

Kay, an experienced high school principal, stated,

> The structure of communication really solidified to be more routine. We'd have a department meeting once a month during a regular school year. That would happen more often now because we had more questions. We had more concerns. We had more work that we had to do in terms of identifying the tools and sharing the tools that were going to make a robust learning experience for students.

The sentiments and experiences principals shared underscore the importance of collective growth mindsets and communication in building team cohesion. The ability to successfully navigate challenges as a team necessitates strong communication planning and implementation. Listening to the community and accurately assessing their communication needs is key. For example, in the excerpt above, Kay demonstrates approaching her school's communication needs with a growth mindset and adapting meeting frequency to address uncertainty and stakeholder concerns.

Distinguishing Factors

There are three important distinguishing factors between a fixed mindset and a growth mindset (Davis, 2019). Leaders who possess growth mindsets exhibit the following three distinguishing factors (Davis, 2019).

- Distinguishing Factor #1: Believe that investing time and effort in a task will lead to growth and development.
- Distinguishing Factor #2: Be willing to face new challenges and see the work through.
- Distinguishing Factor #3: View mistakes as learning lessons.

Let's take a moment to reflect on each of these distinguishing factors. Imagine a time you navigated change. Reflecting on your own perceptions and experiences with that change, consider the following three questions in the self-reflection activity below.

Self-Reflection Activity

1. *Do you believe that your knowledge, skills, and abilities are continuously improving and growing with each new experience?*
2. *Are you willing to face new challenges and see work through to completion?*
3. *Do you view failure and mistakes as opportunities to learn and improve?*

If you said "yes" to these questions, you most likely employ a growth mindset. If you said "no" to these questions, you may find yourself approaching change with a fixed mindset.

Willingness to Face New Challenges and See Work Through to Completion

Dweck (2016) asserts that there are five contexts where possession of a growth mindset makes a significant difference in learning and development, including challenges, obstacles, effort, criticism, and the success of others. Table 2.1 below provides examples of both virtual principal growth mindsets and fixed mindsets in each of these five contexts.

These five contexts certainly played a major role during the pandemic. Principals' transition to virtual principalship posed numerous challenges and obstacles, prompting leaders to assess their own beliefs about change. Would they view the pandemic as an opportunity to develop better systems? Or would they avoid change and hope the learning environment would return to normal?

Principals were also faced with deciding the leadership role they would play in helping others navigate the rapidly changing environment. Would they actively engage in trying new strategies to remove obstacles like insufficient technology or student food insecurity impacting learning and development? Or would they avoid addressing obstacles like these and focus on maintaining practices that worked in the prepandemic environment?

The pandemic also provided a significant opportunity for principals to reflect on the value of their efforts and their responses to criticism, as well as their network of other principals. Principals in the mixed-method study overwhelmingly viewed the virtual principalship as more difficult. However, their

Table 2.1 Virtual Principal Responses in Learning and Development. Adapted from **Dweck (2016),** *Mindset: The New Psychology of Success*

Context	Virtual Principal Responses in Learning and Development	
	Virtual Principal Growth Mindset	Virtual Principal Fixed Mindset
Challenges	Accepts that challenges exist and leads by viewing these challenges as a potential opportunity	Avoids dealing with the challenges and hopes the challenges will disappear or resolve themselves
Obstacles	Sustains leadership through difficulty with a positive focus on removing or overcoming obstacles	Assumes a defensive leadership approach and gives up easily when obstacles emerge
Effort	Maintains motivation and views extra effort as an investment and worthwhile endeavor	Views the investment of extra effort as pointless in the context of the addressing the challenge
Criticism	Uses both positive and negative feedback as a learning opportunity	Uses positive feedback as a learning opportunity, but ignores negative feedback
Success of Others	Views the successes of others as learning and inspiration opportunities	Views the successes of others as threats

perception of this difficult work as worth the effort was central in sustaining a growth mindset approach.

Plenty of opportunities to listen to and learn from criticism and to glean best practice ideas from other principals were also in good supply. Imagine how inundated principals were with complaints and concerns from teachers, parents, and students during the transition to virtual instruction. This abundance of feedback provided a treasure trove of insight into the learning environment as well as suggestions.

Principals with a growth mindset used this feedback to continuously improve operations. Many of principals in the study highlighted the importance of being flexible, adapting based upon feedback, and adopting other principals' successful practices. In other words, the status quo would not work, and principals had to change in order to effectively lead school efforts.

STRATEGIES

Challenges associated with the virtual principalship provide a valuable opportunity for shifting to a growth mindset, investing in professional development, and polishing skills needed for leading effectively in a virtual environment. Jeanes' (2021) research on growth and fixed mindsets in educational environments suggests that growth mindset approaches can be particularly effective in navigating leadership challenges.

In fact, Jeanes's (2021) research argues for integrating growth mindset approaches into educational leadership development at all levels. Fraser (2018) asserts that sustained approaches and embedded efforts are the most effective in fostering long-term development of growth mindsets. Think about teachers who are constantly told they have to adapt to the needs of their students. Why are principals any different?

Imagine if principals had navigated the pandemic with a fixed mindset. What outcomes would we likely see? If educational leaders utilized a fixed mindset during the pandemic, it is possible that many schools would not have been able to pivot to virtual instruction. Without leaders quickly shifting resources to procure needed technology, provide technology training for teachers, and implement virtual instructional leadership, the educational process may have come to a standstill.

Likewise, if principals had not adapted their communications, been flexible, and practiced empathy, there would likely be an even steeper social-emotional toll on teachers, students, and their families from the pandemic. The nation cannot handle a larger teacher shortage, to be honest. Some school districts may have suffered more teacher losses because of the health safety considerations due to the pandemic (Bailey & Schurz, 2020).

Wilson and Conyers (2020) assert there are seven key strategies for developing and sustaining an effective growth mindset over time. These strategies include

1. Understanding differences between growth and fixed mindsets.
2. Considering change through the science of learning growth and development.
3. Being optimistic about learning.
4. Setting personal and organizational growth goals.
5. Seeking feedback needed for improvement.
6. Investing in continuously improving.
7. Focusing on forward progress and the learning journey versus the destination.

The transition to the virtual principalship necessitated all seven of these strategies. In the mixed-method study, principals especially noted the importance of projecting optimism and a sense of calm, investing in continuous improvements, and making forward progress. Perhaps most importantly, the transition to being a virtual principal provided a platform for principals with growth mindsets to model to teachers and students their optimism for learning and view of learning as a lifelong journey.

Dr. Tchiki Davis (2019) suggests that developing a growth mindset can help increase leaders' chances of success. Ascribing to a growth mindset demonstrates the belief that our basic knowledge, skills, and abilities can be continuously improved through professional development, effort, and dedication (Davis, 2019). Insight about our own mindsets helps leaders exert the appropriate amount of individual effort towards accomplishing goals and aspirations (Davis, 2019).

Principals freely expressed they were overwhelmed, anxious, and fear-ridden. However, they learned quickly the need to move forward through team efforts. This philosophy of investing time and effort is consistent and exemplifies the following quote from Dr. Carol Dweck, who coined the growth mindset concept.

The hand you are dealt is just the starting point for development.

—Carol Dweck

Davis (2019) suggests the following fifteen strategies for building a growth mindset:

- Exhibiting the willingness to accept imperfection and opportunities for growth in both ourselves and others.
- Navigating challenges with courage and recognizing that opportunities reside in challenges.
- Paying attention to feelings and the dialogue we choose to use.
- Focusing on positive thoughts and cultivating self-acceptance.
- Taking steps to be an authentic leader seeking your own true goals.
- Fostering a stronger sense of purpose and meaning.
- Exploring and appreciating your own strengths and weaknesses.
- Valuing constructive criticism and using it to make continuous improvements.
- Viewing growth as a journey, not a destination.
- Learning from the experiences of others.
- Recognizing that progress takes time, and that improvement will emerge through practice.

- Taking risks and being willing to encounter mistakes in front of others.
- Being realistic about the amount of time it takes to learn new knowledge, skills, and abilities.
- Focusing on the process versus the amount of time to achieve the desired goal.
- Cultivating resilience and a positive attitude toward sustaining a growth mindset.

Principals drew heavily upon these strategies during their transition to the virtual principalship. The immediacy of the pandemic and enormity of the challenges ahead prompted principals to reflect on their own strengths and weaknesses, accept imperfection, and cultivate self-acceptance. Principals also showed great courage in the face of these challenges, cultivating resilience in teachers, students, and communities.

Ng's (2018) research suggests that leaders' actions are motivated and influenced by intrinsic motivations and that powerful linkages can be made between intrinsic motivation and growth mindsets. Principals are certainly motivated to improve for the sake of those they lead. Change is key to organizational survival and success (Bligh et al., 2018). A leadership focus on fostering risk-taking and embracing employee mistakes lends itself to supporting the development of growth mindsets.

A principal with a growth mindset believes that growth and development can occur through a combination of challenge and support as well as effort, dedication, and hard work. Principals possessing growth mindsets apply this belief to their own professional development and also extend this belief to teachers and students. For example, during the transition to virtual principalship, leaders learned new technologies and also invested in technology training for teachers and school staff.

Ricci (2018) stresses that the first step in developing a growth mindset is for principals to invest time in self-reflection about their own beliefs about academic success and intellectual development. As a principal, this step is critically important as one's own mindset sets the tone for the educational community (Ricci, 2018). Ricci (2018) also highlights the importance of authenticity and congruence between what principals say as leaders and their actions in fostering a community-wide growth mindset philosophy.

Making the choice to be vulnerable and open to potential failure can be difficult. Leaders must develop and embrace an inner trust in themselves to be able to reflect on failures and learn from them in order to grow from them. A growth mindset also requires effort and a commitment to professional development.

With this being said, shouldn't this same mindset continue in a traditional environment? The lessons learned from Covid should transfer. The hope is that teachers and principals as well as district personnel will understand that through mistakes, opportunities for growth are provided and professional development needs are revealed. Without mistakes, opportunities for growth can be limited.

Principals who truly commit to leading with a growth mindset demonstrate to the educational community a deep value and belief in the transformative power of learning and each individual's ability to grow through education. In essence, embracing a growth mindset, enables principals to authentically walk the talk. Table 2.2 below poses key questions to consider and reflect upon in leading with a growth mindset.

Principal's Corner

The following *Principal's Corner* case scenario provides an illustrative example of how a principal employed these strategies to help foster a growth mindset and recognition of the silver lining within a teacher conference in their own educational environment. The case scenario draws upon many

Table 2.2 Virtual Principal Growth Mindset Reflections. *Adapted from Dweck (2016), Mindset: The New Psychology of Success*

Virtual Principal Growth Mindset Reflections	
Context	Growth Mindset
Challenges	• How am I embracing the challenges in my current learning environment? • How can these challenges present opportunities for my organization and students? • How can these challenges be an opportunity for my own professional growth?
Obstacles	• How am I sustaining leadership in the presence of these obstacles? • How can I remove these obstacles or barriers? • How can I overcome these obstacles?
Effort	• How will this effort enhance the learning environment? • Where do I need to focus extra effort? • How am I leading by example through my efforts?
Criticism	• Am I open to both positive and negative feedback? • How do I learn from constructive criticism? • How can I use criticism more effectively in my own professional growth?
Success of Others	• How do I view the successes of others? • What can I learn from the successes of others? • How can I gain inspiration through the successes of others?

strategies for expanding growth mindsets. For example, the strategies in this scenario enabled leaders to better understand teachers' needs and to take action to provide continuous improvement pathways. The scenario also highlights a leadership team's openness to adapt and try new strategies to foster greater organizational success.

> *All educators in America are familiar with RTI or response to intervention for students. RTI is a multitiered approach to the early identification and support of students with learning and behavior needs. RTI is a process that aims to identify kids who are struggling in school and uses targeted teaching to help them catch up. RTI isn't a specific program or teaching method. It's a systematic way of measuring progress and providing more support to kids who need it.*
>
> *Well, we take this systematic approach with our teachers and have RTI for teachers, where we use a targeted approach in meeting their needs or deepening their understanding of a strategy or concern for our students. RTI for teachers is held on Mondays after school beginning at 4 pm and lasts no longer than an hour. Yes, you have heard of RTI for students, but we implemented an RTI for teachers.*
>
> *After many concerns were raised from our special education department (SPED), we decided to meet with a group of teachers to discuss strategies and implementation of certain strategies for our SPED population.*
>
> *We had six teachers, the data demonstrated concern for the SPED teachers and administration. We met with them on Zoom and had the SPED teachers present strategies to the teachers, and you could tell by their body language they were not having it or did not believe the data. The assistant principal and I observed as the teachers were not paying attention. I immediately messaged one of the teachers in the chat box. And before I knew it, I unmuted and expressed to the teachers that this was not a gotcha but for the SPED teachers to model the strategies for them. This is not about you or me but about the students who are three or more grade levels behind. One of the teachers stated, this is not what we did last year, and I followed the strategies from the previous year. I allowed each one of them to vent and then asked the question, What does the data say? Remember, last year was last year, and we have a new group of students and must analyze the situation differently, and we have new SPED teachers. We must work with them and not against them. Now, let's regroup and, with an open mind, listen to the strategies to implement them for our students. We had one teacher request the video, and he watched it three times to reflect on the conversation. He stated that he appreciated the academic feedback and would work with the case manager for his students.*

SUMMARY

This chapter examined how principals navigate challenges associated with virtual principalship and the perception of the role as more difficult and time intensive than leading in traditional face-to-face educational environments. These challenges necessitated additional knowledge, skills, and abilities for effective virtual leadership. The challenges also provided a valuable opportunity for shifting to a growth mindset, investing in professional development, and polishing skills needed for effective virtual principalship.

POLISHING THE DIAMOND

1. What is a growth mindset?
2. What is a fixed mindset?
3. What three factors distinguish a growth mindset from a fixed mindset?
4. What were three silver linings of the transition to the virtual principalship?
5. What are strategies for transitioning from a fixed mindset to a growth mindset? Give examples.
6. Explain how principals' growth mindsets influence the mindsets of teachers and students in the educational environment.
7. Describe five contexts where a growth mindset makes a significant difference in learning and development.
8. List three strategies principals can use to strengthen their own growth mindsets.
9. How can districts support principals in fostering growth mindsets? List three ways.

REFERENCES

Bailey, J. P., & Schurz, J. (2020). COVID-19 Is Creating a School Personnel Crisis. *American Enterprise Institute*. ERIC Number: ED606250

Bligh, M. C., Kohles, J. C., & Yan. Q. (2018). Leading and Learning to Change: The Role of Leadership Style and Mindset in Error Learning and Organizational Change. *Journal of Change Management*, 18(2), 116–141.

Davis, T. (2019). 15 Ways to Build a Growth Mindset. *Psychology Today*, Retrieved https://www.psychologytoday.com/us/blog/click-here-happiness/201904/15-ways-build-growth-mindset?eml

Dweck, C. (2006). *Mindset: The Psychology of* Success. New York: Random House.

Dweck, C. (2014). Developing a Growth Mindset. Retrieved from http://www.youtube.com/watch?v=hiiEeMN7vbQ

Fraser, D. M. (2018). An Exploration of the Application and Implementation of Growth Mindset Principles within a Primary School. *British Journal of Educational Psychology*, 88(4), 645–658.

Jeanes, E. (2021). A Meeting of Mind(sets): Integrating the Pedagogy and Andragogy of Mindsets for Leadership Development. *Thinking Skills and Creativity*, 39.

Ng, B. (2018). The Neuroscience of Growth Mindset and Intrinsic Motivation. *Brain Sciences*, 8(2), 20–27.

Ricci, M. C. (2018). *Create a Growth Mindset School: An Administrator's Guide to Leading a Growth Mindset Community*. Waco, TX: Prufrock Press.

Seaton, F. S. (2018). Empowering Teachers to Implement a Growth Mindset. *Educational Psychology in Practice*, 34(1), 41–57.

Wilson, D., & Conyers, M. (2020). *Developing Growth Mindsets: Principles and Practices for Maximizing Students' Potential*. Alexandria, VA: ASCD.

Chapter 3

Communication and Presence

The art of communication is the language of leadership.

—James Humes

NATURE OF VIRTUAL LEARNING

The twenty-four-hour-a-day, seven day-a-week nature of virtual learning blurs traditional time and communication pathways, necessitating intentional virtual communication strategies (Joosten et al., 2020). Principals must intentionally design communication strategies that are frequent, accurate, clear, and effective in meeting the information needs of teachers and staff, students and their families, and other school stakeholders.

Ferrell and Kline (2018) assert that effective communication and building trust are even more critical in remote learning environments. The nature of virtual learning also prompts the use of technology in communication and necessitates the creation of a strong sense of leader presence. Leadership presence is especially essential in the virtual learning environment since the school community is distributed and connected via technology versus being physically present in a centralized learning environment.

Imagine the early stages of the Covid-19 pandemic and the countless questions students and their families had about attending school, virtual instruction, and technology. Now add to that the innumerable questions posed by teachers and school staff about the transition to virtual instruction, technology, student accountability and discipline, and best practices in student engagement. What would have happened if principals had not increased their communications and sense of presence to help answer those questions? Principals immediately sensed the need for an increase in their leadership communications and presence.

NAVIGATING EXPECTATIONS

In the individual interview component, all ten principals and superintendents identified the ability to demonstrate a strong sense of presence and sustain frequent communications as critical expectations in the virtual principal role. Therefore, 100 percent of the research participants viewed communication strategies as paramount in their perception of virtual principal effectiveness. The ability to navigate different expectations for presence and communication associated with the twenty-four/seven nature of virtual learning is represented by the comments of a current principal highlighted below. Melanie, an experienced high school principal, notes the importance of delivery and overcoming communication barriers as a virtual leader, noting the importance of strengthening "active listening. We all need to listen to one another." Christina, a school superintendent with extensive experience, also notes the importance of considering the delivery of communications in the virtual environment by noting,

> Your mannerisms and your voice, sometimes it can be misconstrued. You have to be really careful not to sound too enthusiastic; otherwise you sound aggressive. . . . You have to control your style and delivery.

In the quantitative component of the mixed-methods study, principals and superintendents reported significant professional development needs in communicating as a leader in the virtual environment. In fact, the overwhelming majority of principals and superintendents ranked every communication-related virtual principal learning outcome domain as a moderate to very high need.

Professional development in understanding how to rally a community in a virtual environment and understanding how to communicate with staff and students in a virtual environment were the two highest communication-related learning domain areas, with over 84 percent of all principals and superintendents reporting moderate to very high support needs in both of these areas.

Over 71 percent of all principals in the study also reported the need for additional professional development in understanding how to communicate with difficult teachers in a virtual environment. Districts should heed this advice and establish communication professional development in which principals develop communication systems. A systems approach will ensure increased and continuous communication.

PREVENTING COMMUNICATION BARRIERS

Communication is an essential component of leadership for virtual principals and is critical to success in leading within virtual learning environments (Simmons, 2020). Communication barriers are often more common in virtual settings (Ferrell & Kline, 2018; Strikowsky, 2020). Therefore, virtual principals must invest time in effectively communicating and preventing communication barriers (Simmons, 2020).

First and Carr (1986) assert that principals can significantly improve their communications with teachers and build trust by removing communication barriers. Communication barriers occur when there is a disruption in the ability to convey a message or for a message to be effectively received. Guarding against these disruptions is especially important for principals communicating within the virtual environment.

There are four major categories of communication barriers that commonly impact messages in virtual learning environments: process, personal, physical, and semantic barriers (Simmons, 2020). Ensuring teachers are aware of organizational information and resources helps prevent personal and semantic barriers (First & Carr, 1986). This is critical to developing trust, which is especially important in times of great change or challenge.

Process barriers include disruptions in the process of transmitting or receiving the message itself. For example, consider an instance where a virtual principal believes they sent a communication to all teachers, but the email server failed to transmit the message. Process barriers also occur when there are breakdowns in the systems approach to communication.

Personal barriers include individual characteristics or beliefs that disrupt the message from being accurately transmitted or received. For example, consider a principal whose listening skills resulted in only half of a message being received. Or consider a virtual principal who does not fully understand their stakeholders. Miscommunication is just as problematic as no communication.

Physical barriers include factors in the physical environment that prevent the message from being communicated as intended. For example, envision an online teaching professional development session that is conducted in an auditorium with significant nearby construction noise disrupting key messages from being heard. Or consider professional development with a large audience, in which only half of the teachers are focused.

Semantic barriers involve communication difficulties due to language or differences in interpretation. For example, imagine a virtual principal who communicates to teachers that student attendance reports are needed right away. This message is likely to be interpreted differently, with some teachers making it their first task, others sending the report by the end of the day, and others viewing "right away" as by the end of the week. Specificity is necessary.

Effective communication entails constantly monitoring for communication barriers and employing strategies to prevent them. Considering each of the four major categories of potential communication barriers can be helpful in maintaining awareness and developing prevention strategies. For example, a virtual principal with an important message to send to the learning community might ask themselves the following questions:

1. What steps can I take to help ensure the process of transmitting and receiving the message is effective? (*Process Communication Barriers*)
2. How have I considered the intended audience in the development of the message? *(Personal Communication Barriers)*
3. Are there any adjustments to the physical or technological environment that would make the message delivery more effective? *(Physical Communication Barriers)*
4. Have I created the message using understandable language that is free from jargon and slang? Does the message include all specifics needed? *(Semantic Communication Barriers)*

Additional strategies for preventing communication barriers are provided in Table 3.1.

Hill and Bartol's (2018) study on effective communication strategies in virtual organizations found there are five best practices for improving communication in remote work teams. Hill and Bartol (2018) suggest the following five steps leaders should take to enhance communications in the virtual environment:

1. Aligning appropriate technologies to the work task
2. Establishing clear goals
3. Synchronizing action steps
4. Being supportive
5. Maintaining open and inclusive communication channels

These five steps were critical to success during the transition to the virtual principalship. In the study, principals highlighted the vital role task alignment, goal setting, and planning action steps played in moving their organizations forward. They also emphasized the importance of demonstrating empathy and support, expanding communication, and demonstrating presence.

Table 3.1 Strategies for Preventing Communication Barriers

Communication Barriers	Strategies for Preventing Communication Barriers
Process Barriers	• Utilizing different communication pathways • Tailoring the communication medium to best fit the intended message • Clarifying the message to help ensure understanding • Seeking feedback to enhance understanding • Confirming receipt of messages
Personal Barriers	• Utilizing active listening skills • Understanding the audience • Tailoring the message to the audience • Building trust • Studying cultural differences
Physical Barriers	• Redesigning physical spaces to enhance communication • Considering time zones • Expanding technology access • Reducing environmental noise and distractions • Ensuring technology functionality
Semantic Barriers	• Using clear and simple terminology • Avoiding words with multiple meanings • Translating terminology • Defining acronyms • Avoiding jargon and slang • Providing sufficient details

PRESENCE IN THE VIRTUAL ENVIRONMENT

Baldoni (2009) describes leadership presence in terms of earned authority, respect, and trust. Presence is built through demonstrating competence and the capability to connect with other people (Baldoni, 2009). This sense of leadership presence is especially important in the virtual environment. In virtual environments, physical proximity is often limited, necessitating that leaders take intentional steps to demonstrate presence remotely.

Virtual principals are facing heightened internal and external expectations to demonstrate a stronger sense of presence in the virtual educational environment. Melanie, a high school principal with extensive experience, states as a virtual principal she "doesn't have an office; the school is my office." Similarly, Jack, a first-year principal, reports he frequently "pops into online classes to show visibility" and states, "Communication in the virtual environment should be more. It's more important because we don't have these students in the building." John, a high school principal with four years of experience, shares that this sense of presence also needs to extend to the local community through the following sentiment: "Being a rock or a cornerstone for the community. I did as much food delivery in the spring as I did instructional leadership. . . . It was a reminder to the community that we are present and still here." Principals in the study shared how their communities looked to them as leaders during the Covid-19 pandemic. Principals found themselves not only providing instructional leadership within the school environment, but also serving actively within their communities. Principals highlighted examples of delivering food or setting up food distribution centers to address food insecurity and the disruption of school breakfast and lunch service. Some principals even walked door to door in their communities to communicate with and assess the needs of students and families.

Tomlinson (2014) provides the following description of a principal with exemplary leadership presence in the following excerpt,

> He found a place in the hallways through which almost every person in the school passes during the course of a typical day. He makes it a priority to stand at that spot whenever people are moving about. This allows him to connect with nearly everyone every day. The principal who stood in the hallway was creating an opportunity to act as a symbolic and cultural leader. By seeing colleagues and students daily, creating opportunities to initiate conversations that helped him understand their concerns and communicate his own vision for the school. (p. 90)

Sergiovanni (1999) argues that symbolic and cultural leadership is especially powerful in creating a strong sense of community and focusing the organization on achieving its mission. Principals' support for their communities during the pandemic demonstrated both symbolic and cultural leadership principles.

Mockler (2020) asserts that leadership presence comprises several key components, including the ability to lead various audiences and stakeholders, communicate ideas with confidence, demonstrate professionalism, and appropriately balance talking and listening. Several key strategies for enhancing leadership presence include enhancing confidence by using posture and body language, observing and learning from other leaders who demonstrate a strong sense of presence, and seeking feedback from trusted colleagues (Mockler, 2020).

Mockler's (2020) research argues that striking the right balance between talking and listening is often the most difficult aspect of leadership presence. Achieving the appropriate balance of talking and listening is a moving target, requiring constant adaptation, situational awareness, and the ability to correctly read the environment (Mockler, 2020).

Imagine sitting in a Zoom session with teachers in the early stages of the pandemic. What would happen if the virtual principal talked during the whole session? The virtual principal would most likely miss critical opportunities to gain insight about how teachers were feeling and their needs. The principal would also likely miss the opportunity to convey empathy and fully address stakeholder concerns.

Principal's Corner

The following *Principal's Corner* case scenario provides an illustrative example of "reading the situation" and knowing how to support teachers based upon that "read."

> *My mother has always told my sisters and me that body language will inform you of everything. So you must be aware of your surroundings and nonbody language too. One scenario where I "read" the situation and offered support was about our SPED department. The two teachers were conversing back and forth and not paying attention to each other or what they were saying. My assistant principal, Melanie McGrath, said, "Dickson, we might have a situation on our hands with the two teachers." After reading the emails and listening to Melanie, I picked up on the vibes and clues of the two teachers not collaborating, on the same page, feeling upset and intense with each other.*
>
> *We called them in for a Zoom meeting with a Pear Deck presentation. Now, Pear Deck is a Google add-on where teachers can present the content to the students and ask questions for the students to answer and receive immediate academic feedback. From there, we organized a sit-down with both teachers and had the agenda and questions ready. I recall the first question; the teacher unmuted herself to answer the question. I said, "No, please take sixty seconds to reflect and answer the question." They took their time and wrote the responses, and when the time was up, their answers were displayed side by side to discuss deeper.*
>
> *We didn't just straight mediate between the two teachers, but we offered support via Pear Deck. The presentation allowed them to share their opinions and perspectives and not only hear but visually see each other's responses side by side. When there were inconsistencies or disagreements, they could work through those. In the end, the SPED teachers built a collaborative plan with no emotional baggage to service our students and increase their capacity as SPED teachers and colleagues.*

FREQUENCY OF COMMUNICATIONS

Virtual principals are also facing increased expectations to sustain more frequent communications. When asked about the knowledge, skills, and abilities needed by virtual principals, Kay, an experienced high school principal, states,

> What I did find from the leadership position was how important it was to be accessible almost round the clock, twenty-four/seven, to faculty, to staff, to parents, and even to students. I made sure that all of my school community had my cell phone. . . . I'd begin at least 6:30 in the morning and usually did not end until 10:30 at night in terms of communication. And that would be individual communication but also beginning immediately routinized at least weekly if not biweekly communication with parents and with faculty and staff.

It is important to note that many principals highlighted the emotional toll and exhaustion resulting from these expanded communication and presence expectations.

Schmidt's (2014) research on virtual leadership suggests that increased frequency of communications as well as a focus on relationship building is essential in building effective virtual teams. This was certainly the case in the transition to virtual principalship during the pandemic. Virtual principals noted increased team cohesion as a result of their expanded communications and focus on relationship building.

SUMMARY

Insight is offered into the heightened internal and external expectations for virtual principals to demonstrate a stronger sense of presence and sustain more frequent communications. The twenty-four/seven nature of virtual learning blurs traditional time and communication pathways, necessitating intentional virtual communication strategies. A discussion of best practices and strategies for effectively navigating stakeholder expectations, preventing communication barriers, and increasing the perception of presence and frequency of communications is provided.

POLISHING THE DIAMOND

1. What is a communication barrier?
2. Describe four types of communication barriers.
3. Which communication barriers are most common in your own organization? Why?
4. What strategies can be used to overcome communication barriers?
5. What strategies can you use to demonstrate leadership presence in the virtual environment?
6. Explain the importance of leadership presence for stakeholders in the educational environment.

7. What strategies can you use to demonstrate effective communication in the virtual environment?
8. List three strategies principals can use to increase their communication frequency.
9. How can districts support principals in demonstrating increased presence and communications? List two ways.

REFERENCES

Avolio, B., & Kahai, S. (2003). Adding the "E" to E-leadership: How It May Impact Your Leadership. *Organizational Dynamics,* 31(4), 325–338.

Baldoni, J. (2009). Developing Your Leadership Presence. *Harvard Business Review,* October 21, 2009. Accessed https://hbr.org/2009/10/developing-your-leadership-pres

Ferrell, J., & Kline, K. (2018). Facilitating Trust and Communication in Virtual Teams. *People & Strategy,* 41(2).

First, P. F., & Carr, D. S. (1986). Removing Barriers to Communication between Principals and Teachers. *Catalyst for Change,* 15(3), 5–7.

Hill, N. S., & Bartol, K. M. (2018). Five Ways to Improve Communication in Virtual Teams. *Management Review,* 60(1). Accessed https://sloanreview.mit.edu/issue/2018-fall/

Joosten, T., Lee-McCarthy, K., Harness, L., & Paulus, R. (2020). *Digital Learning Innovation Trends.* Online Learning Consortium. ERIC Number: ED603277

Mockler, S. (2020). Leadership Presence: Define it, Develop It, and Use It. Accessed https://www.vantageleadership.com/our-blog/leadership-presence-define-develop-use/

Schmidt, G. B. (2014). Virtual Leadership: An Important Leadership Context. *Industrial and Organizational Psychology,* 7(2), 182–187.

Sergiovanni, T. (1999). *Rethinking leadership.* Glenview, IL: Skylight.

Simmons, J. M. (2020). *Perception Is Reality: Teachers" Perceptions of the Presence of Servant Leadership Characteristics in Public School Principals and Its Influence on Teachers.* https://inspire.redlands.edu/work/ns/6b0ff8cb-7cf0-4239-8d0c-55f5e2432521

Strikowsky, O. (2020). *Enhancing Workplace Communication during the Pandemic and Beyond.* Cornell University School of Industrial and Labor Relations. Accessed https://www.ilr.cornell.edu/work-and-coronavirus/student-voices/enhancing-workplace-communication-during-pandemic-and-beyond

Tomlinson, C. A. (2014). One to Grow On / The Principal in the Hallway, *Educational Leadership,* 71(6), 90–91.

Chapter 4

Projecting Calm

The true measure of leadership is staying calm in the storm.

—Marty Fukuda

CONVEYING A SENSE OF CALM

The Covid-19 pandemic placed principals directly in the eye of the storm, necessitating not only the transition to the "virtual principalship," but also the new responsibility of leading their learning communities through the crisis. As part of their crisis leadership, principals actively attended to the social-emotional needs of employees, students, and their communities (Anderson, Hayes, & Carpenter, 2020; Kaul, VanGronigen, & Simon, 2020).

Witnessing many teachers, staff, students, and parents struggling with fear of the Covid-19 virus as well as its related impacts on daily life, principals projected a sense of calm to moderate some of the fear (Anderson, Hayes, & Carpenter, 2020). Principals' frequent communications and calm leadership were essential in creating a sense of consistency during school closures (Anderson, Hayes, & Carpenter, 2020; Kaul, VanGronigen, & Simon, 2020).

Because principals were faced with a monumental leadership challenge and at the same time were heavily engaged in caring for others during the Covid-19 pandemic, they experienced pronounced levels of stress (Anderson, Hayes, & Carpenter, 2020). Leaders' stress and anxiety can often be perceived throughout the workplace environment (Levin, 2018). In fact, employees perceive leaders as ineffective or harmful if they are unable to constructively manage their own stress.

Therefore, it is essential for leaders to exercise self-care and stress management in order to lead with a sense of calmness. Levin (2018) asserts mindfulness enhances leaders' ability to manage their own stress, which translates to reducing employee stress and creating a healthier work environment. Furthermore, when leaders utilize mindfulness practices, organizations experience increases in hope, optimism, self-efficacy, and resilience (Levin, 2018).

Levin (2018) argues there are two key characteristics of mindful leaders:

1. The ability to separate their personal feelings about stressful challenges and view challenges from an objective position.
2. The capability to moderate and delay their reactions to challenges in order to invest time in reflecting on possible options and strategies.

Emotional energy is modeled by leaders to their employees, emphasizing the importance of engaging in mindfulness practices including fostering self-awareness, reminding oneself of the importance of remaining objective, engaging in meditation and exercise, and scheduling relaxation time (Anderson, Hayes, & Carpenter, 2020; Levin, 2018).

Principals also reported the value of networking and staying connected to other principals in mitigating their stress (Anderson, Hayes, & Carpenter, 2020). In times of crisis and great change there is often limited time. Principals created efficiencies by not re-creating the wheel. They shared best practices, used each other as sounding boards for new ideas, and provided self-care recommendations to one another.

Marty Fukuda (2015) asserts there are four essential strategies for projecting calm and leading in challenging times. Fukuda (2015) describes the following key strategies:

- **Keeping a calm mind.** When the going gets tough, leaders and teams need to remain focused. Leaders who project confidence and a calm demeanor, regardless of the emotions they are feeling, can better refocus team efforts on the goal versus fear.
- **Being extremely transparent.** Communicating honestly with employees about challenges helps keep the team focused on the work ahead. Providing information to help employees fully understand the situation enables employees to share their great ideas and to rally to help the organization navigate the challenges.
- **Communicating an inspirational vision.** During challenging times, a unifying vision is extraordinarily valuable in maintaining team focus toward goal attainment. It is also essential to celebrate small and large team gains to further propel team momentum.
- **Focusing on being proactive.** While some short-term quick reactions may be necessary, the faster leaders are able to shift teams back to

focusing on proactive actions will create a long-term organizational advantage.

Principals navigating the transition to the virtual principalship during the Covid-19 pandemic drew heavily upon these four strategies. Principals quickly found that stakeholders in their learning communities expected increased communication and presence and relied on them to project a sense of calm. Embracing a growth mindset, principals focused on taking each day at a time, driving their organizations to make steady forward progress while focusing on student success.

The capability for virtual principals to project calm during uncertainty was a critical skill identified by the overwhelming majority of interview participants in the study. Kay, an experienced high school principal, notes the importance of providing encouragement and constantly communicating to teachers "you can do this" and further elaborates,

> We have to be the anxiety relievers in chief. . . . We have to be the calm voice of reason, the person who does not devolve into hysteria, but keeps the steady hand, keeps even keel as communication comes down to us from the state or district and get that out and interpret it. . . . Communication has been frustrating for teachers. They read things in the newspaper. They read things on the state department website. They listen to the board meetings. Who is pulling all that together for them and keeping the calm focus on student learning? That has to be the principal more than ever. More than ever.

Hanna, an experienced high school principal, describes the transition to virtual learning,

> Teachers were thinking we'll be back in a month. And then a month turned into two months and that's when I really began to see the just sheer fear in them. It was fear. [Teachers were saying] I don't think I can do this. I don't know how to do this. I had to keep telling them we are in this together. We are all going to make mistakes but in the forefront always is what is in the best interest of children and we have grace, we care about our kids, and we make sure they are safe. That's our big priority right now.

Bell, a secondary principal with five years of experience, shares how important the ability to "spend time reassuring others it was possible" was to the learning environment. John, a high school principal with four years of experience, also shares this sentiment in the following statement: "Having stability to cope with and deal with uncertainty, flexibility, and stress, was essential and to process it, absorb it, and project out calm to your staff."

PRINCIPAL'S CORNER

The following *Principal's Corner* provides practical tips for projecting calm in the midst of a storm. As you review these tips, reflect on a challenge you have faced. How might these steps help navigate that challenge?

As you are going through the storm,

- *Verify that it is a storm.*
- *See what type of storm it is. Hurricanes are very different than a tornado or tsunami.*
- *Listen to the storm.*
- *Ask questions about how the storm began.*
- *Ask more questions and see what the data says about which direction the storm is trying to go. (Sometimes you do not want to venture in that direction.)*
- *Breathe and ask more questions to prompt further reflection.*

NATURE OF CHANGE

Fullan (2002) differentiates between leaders who have innovative ideas and leaders who truly understand the change process. This differentiation is valuable because being an effective leader and change agent requires gaining buy-in and commitment from stakeholders who may hold differing perspectives (Fullan, 2002).

> *Only principals who are equipped to handle a complex, rapidly changing environment can implement the reforms that lead to sustained improvement in student achievement.*
>
> —Michael Fullan

Truly understanding the change process and gaining buy-in from stakeholders was especially important during the pandemic. Principals faced an unprecedented challenge with many layers of complexity in the decision-making process. Utilizing a systemic change management process was critically important in successfully transitioning their schools to virtual instruction, meeting stakeholder needs, and making the changes sustainable.

Harvard business professor John Kotter's (1996) book *Leading Change* presents a comprehensive change management model that has been widely used throughout business and industry, nonprofit and governmental sectors, and educational institutions. Kotter's model focuses on how stakeholders feel about the change as well as their engagement in the change process (Kotter, 1996, 1999, 2007; Kotter & Cohen, 2002). The model's consideration of stakeholder feelings is congruent with leadership efforts to project calmness. The model delineates eight key steps for effectively leading change and engaging stakeholders in the change process. The eight steps in Kotter's (1996) model are depicted in Figure 4.1.

During the pandemic, principals utilizing Kotter's (1996) model communicated to their stakeholders the urgency to prepare and transition to virtual instruction to ensure continuity of instruction. They formed coalitions who helped plan for future changes. Principals also created a compelling vision for making forward progress, communicated the vision, and removed obstacles to empower others to act upon the vision. They also celebrated short-term wins, while recognizing there was still significant work to be done. Principals also utilized systems approaches to anchor the changes into their school's culture to make them more sustainable over time.

Fullan (2002) recommends the following leadership guidelines for truly understanding and leading change processes.

1. Innovate selectively in alignment with organizational goals.
2. Realize innovative ideas are not sufficient. Leaders must help others understand and commit to the ideas.

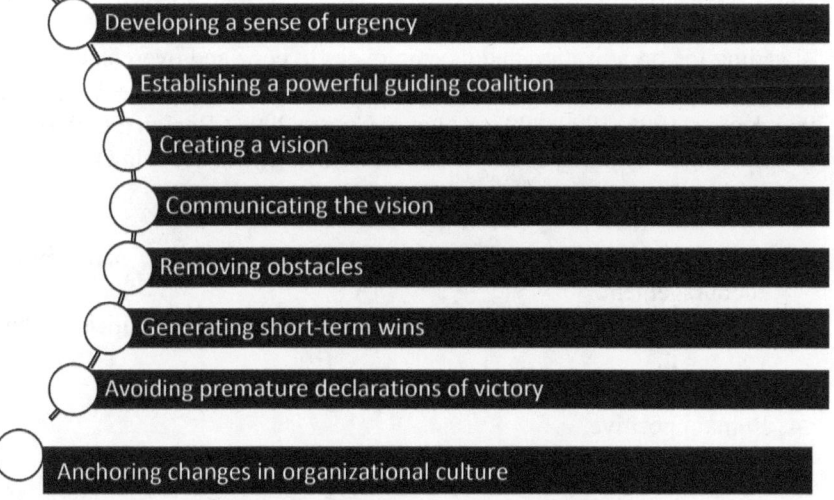

Figure 4.1 Kotter's (1996) Eight-Step Change Management Model

3. Anticipate and appreciate challenges that arise while implementing new ideas.
4. Embrace, learn, and find strategies to address constructive criticism.
5. Focus on transforming organizational culture as it leads to longer lasting change.
6. Recognize that change is complex and requires a significant investment of time and effort.

During the transition to the virtual principalship, leaders realized they must be selective and intentional with their actions and resources. Alignment to student success required focused efforts, stakeholder buy-in, and commitment. Principals in the study highlighted the importance of learning and trying new strategies, being open to criticism and feedback, and investing significant time in the change management process.

REASSURANCE, ENCOURAGEMENT AND MOTIVATION

Virtual principals provide critical reassurance, encouragement, and motivation throughout the learning community by projecting calm and effectively managing change (Jennings et al., 2019). Change can be challenging, disruptive, stressful, and quite unsettling for many employees and organizations (Jennings et al., 2019; Ranjan, 2020). Ranjan (2020) highlights that utilizing a change management process with appropriate coping and support strategies helps make supervision easier when the organization is navigating tumultuous change.

Leading the organization and its employees to cope and overcome change anxiety takes significant time and investment (Anderson, Hayes, & Carpenter, 2020; Kotter, 1996, 1999, 2007; Kotter & Cohen, 2002). Ranjan (2020) offers the following five strategies for leaders to aid employees in coping with organizational change:

1. Listen to employees, observe their change experience, and provide encouragement.
2. Demonstrate to employees that you care and recognize resilience when you see it.
3. Make improvements employees recommend when possible.
4. Remain positive.
5. Prepare and train employees for the change.

Principals in the study utilized a wide variety of techniques to implement these five strategies. For example, principals used weekly staff meetings, individual conferences, Zoom sessions, observations, and professional development sessions as opportunities to listen to employees, learn about their experiences, and provide recognition and encouragement. Principals also projected calm, optimism, and reassurance through demonstrating empathy.

In times of crisis and change, teacher stress and burnout heighten and become a concerning issue leaders must address (Richards, 2007). Ingersoll (2001) postulates that the level of principal support is one of the most critical factors in whether teachers are retained and persevere. To be most effective, principals must be aware of the type of support their teachers need and value (Richards, 2007).

Richard's (2007) research on teacher perspectives on principal behavior suggests there are differences in how principals and teachers rate teacher support needs. According to Richard (2007), teachers rate the top five principal support behaviors as

1. Respecting and valuing teachers.
2. Providing support for teachers in student discipline.
3. Being present and maintaining an open-door policy.
4. Demonstrating fairness, honesty, and trust.
5. Providing support for teacher interactions with parents.

Recognition of teacher needs during the pandemic was especially important as the quick pivot to virtual instruction and uncertainty of the pandemic created a significant social and emotional toll on teachers. During the study, principals shared the importance of demonstrating even more respect, care, and support for teachers as they navigated the pandemic as a team. More frequent communications, presence, and backup for student discipline and parental interactions were key strategies principals used to demonstrate this commitment to teachers.

The utilization of each step of Kotter's Eight-Step Change Management Model can also help ensure principals are reflecting on employees', students', and community stakeholder's reassurance, encouragement, and motivation needs within each stage of the change process. Addressing stakeholder feelings in the change process is critically important and essential in making the changes sustainable (Kotter, 1996, 1999, 2007; Kotter & Cohen, 2002).

Strategies for incorporating stakeholder reassurance, encouragement, and motivation within the change process are depicted in Table 4.1.

Several commonalities emerged during the study in terms of how principals navigated the change process. As principals created a sense of urgency for preparing for the transition to virtual instruction, they focused upon what

Table 4.1 Kotter's Eight-Step Change Management Model and Virtual Principal Strategies. Adapted from J. P. Kotter (1996), *Leading Change*

Kotter's Eight-Step Change Management Model	
Change Steps	**Virtual Principal Strategies**
Developing a sense of urgency	• Be transparent and fully communicate the need for change. • Provide data and examples to help explain and reassure others why the change is needed right away and what may happen if changes are not made. • Personalize the change and translate the change in terms of what it means to stakeholders.
Establishing a powerful guiding coalition	• Engage stakeholders from throughout the organization, both critics and advocates. • Include individuals with different sources of power (institutional knowledge power, expert power, position authority power). • Publicize the establishment of the guiding coalition throughout the organization so people know how stakeholder voices and recommendations are being integrated.
Creating a vision	• Develop a specific vision for the organization. • Engage the guiding coalition and other stakeholder groups in the creation of that vision. • Encourage stakeholders to participate in the development of the vision and invite them to express their feelings in the process.
Communicating the vision	• Widely communicate the vision throughout the organization and community. • Use the vision to reassure, encourage, and motivate stakeholders about the future. • Utilize different communication channels and mediums to ensure stakeholder receipt and understanding of the message.
Removing obstacles	• Listen to stakeholders and observe their change experience to identify potential roadblocks. • Demonstrate to stakeholders the willingness to listen as well as adjust policies and procedures that will help facilitate the desired change. • Encourage stakeholders to propose new ideas or ways of operating that remove obstacles in the work environment.

Generating short-term wins	• Take the time to celebrate small successes and reassure stakeholders about progress and the future. • Recognize individual stakeholder and collective successes. • Reward resilience
Avoiding premature declarations of victory	• Communicate the long-term sustainability of the changes. • Engage stakeholders in setting both short-term and long-term individual and organizational goals. • Motivate employees to participate in strategic planning and professional development.
Anchoring change in organizational culture	• Communicate about the changes frequently. • Integrate the changes in multiple institutionalized processes (for example, funding justifications, strategic planning, and personnel goals and evaluations) to ensure sustainability and making the changes part of daily organizational life. • Talk about the journey and challenges overcome, and celebrate successes.

was best for students and tried to let that key tenet guide their actions. They also assessed their organizations to identify personnel who had strong technology skills who could aid others during the transition process. Another key commonality was expansion of their current communications strategies to address stakeholders' concerns and needs.

LEARNING AS THE FOCAL POINT

Effective principals are central to leading their organizations through large-scale, sustainable change processes that center learning as the focal point. Fullan (2002) highlights that effective principals must also focus on making coherence out of changes the organization is experiencing. Leaders can draw upon their mission and purpose, understanding of organizational change, collaboration with colleagues, and the knowledge sharing practices to help foster a deeper sense of coherence in the midst of change (Fullan, 2002).

For example, principals in the study highlighted the importance of networking with other principals to learn new strategies and best practices that could be shared within their schools. Principals also emphasized the role they assumed in interpreting district polices and guidance as well as information flowing from the state department of education and news services in order to clarify conflicting guidance that emerged in the early stages of the pandemic.

The process of creating coherence provides a valuable opportunity to focus on student learning and achievement as the central, most important element of educational change (Fullan, 2002). Coherence can also help the school community and other stakeholders look toward the future and achieve greater alignment with the desired goals and vision (Fullan, 2002). For example, principals refocused their learning communities on asking one question: What is best for our students?

SUMMARY

This chapter focused on the importance of virtual principals conveying a sense calm during uncertainty. Navigating change presents unique challenges within the culture of educational organizations as well as significant implications for the morale of school employees, students and their families, and community stakeholders. This chapter provides a robust discussion of specific strategies for conveying calmness through reassurance, encouragement, and motivation, while ensuring student learning remains the focal point.

POLISHING THE DIAMOND

1. What are advantages associated with leaders projecting calm during times of challenge? Give examples.
2. What are two characteristics of mindful leaders?
3. Describe four essential strategies for projecting calm and leading in challenging times.
4. What are three practical steps for projecting calm in the midst of a crisis?
5. Describe the steps in Kotter's Eight-Step Change Management Model.
6. What strategies can principals use to implement Kotter's Eight-Step Change Management Model? Describe three.
7. What strategies can principals use to reassure and encourage others during challenging situations?
8. How can virtual principals motivate others by projecting calm in crisis situations?
9. How can districts support principals in projecting calm during challenges? List two examples.

REFERENCES

Anderson, E., Hayes, S., & Carpenter, B. (2020). Principal as Caregiver of All: Responding to Needs of Others and Self. *CPRE Policy Briefs.* Accessed https://repository.upenn.edu/cpre_policybriefs/92

Fukuda, M. (2015). The True Measure of Leadership Is Staying Calm in the Storm. *Entrepreneur.* Accessed https://www.entrepreneur.com/article/253116#

Fullan, M. (2002). The Change Leader. *Educational Leadership*, 59(8), 16–21.

Ingersoll, R. M. (2001). Teacher Turnover and Teacher Shortages: An Organizational Analysis. *American Educational Research Journal*, 38(3), 499–534.

Jennings, P. A., Jennings, P. A., DeMauro, A. A., & Mischenko, P. P. (2019). *The Mindful School: Transforming School Culture through Mindfulness and Compassion.* New York: Guilford Press.

Kaul, M., VanGronigen, B. A., & Simon, N. S. (2020). Calm during Crisis: School Principal Approaches to Crisis Management during the COVID-19 Pandemic. *CPRE Policy Briefs.* Accessed https://repository.upenn.edu/cpre_policybriefs/89

Kotter, J. P. (2007). Leading Change: Why Transformation Efforts Fail. *Harvard Business Review*, 1, 2–9.

Kotter, J. P. (1999). *John Kotter on What Leaders Really Do.* Boston: Harvard Business School Press.

Kotter, J. P. (1996). *Leading Change.* Boston: Harvard Business School Press.

Kotter, J. P., & Cohen, D. S. (2002). *The Heart of Change.* Boston: Harvard Business School Press

Levin, M. (2018). *Mindful Leaders Develop Better Companies and Happier Employees.* INC Publishing.

Ranjan, R. (2020). *Five Powerful Ways to Help Your Employees Cope with Change.* INC Publishing.

Richards, J. (2007). *How Effective Principals Encourage Their Teachers.* National Association of Elementary School Principals. Accessed https://www.naesp.org/sites/default/files/resources/2/Principal/2007/J-Fp48.pdf

Chapter 5

Technology

Technology is best when it brings people together.

—Matt Mullenweg

TECHNOLOGY AND THE VIRTUAL PRINCIPAL

During the Covid-19 pandemic, the whole world was thrust into using technology daily with remote working due to shutdowns (Kniffin et al., 2021). Most schoolteachers and administrators were not excluded. Though many schools possessed the technology needed, some did not. Even among those schools that did have technology in place, the daily use of technology to provide the entirety of instruction in an engaging manner was not the norm. Williamson, Eynon, and Potter (2020) stated,

> There is no simple mapping of offline onto online that can escape the essential disjuncture between what is possible and what is impossible under these circumstances, no matter how many times parents and/or educators are told that it is easy and that the "digital" makes it so. (p. 111)

Educators certainly found this to be true. Teachers, many of whom have never taught online, were forced to abruptly shift 100 percent of instruction to an online environment, but that was not all. This shift required teachers to redesign their curriculum practices to include a plethora of new technologies (Gurley, 2018); furthermore, not only did teachers need to learn how to teach in this environment, but they also needed to learn how to support learning in a virtual world.

These two different concepts, when combined, were foreign to most. As a result, teachers needed support and a common view of instructional expectations for virtual learning and teaching (Howard et al., 2020). These needs have to be addressed by the principal, and they have to be addressed in a timely fashion. Leaving instructional expectations unclear results in many inequitable opportunities for students.

Just as teachers may not have been prepared for the unforeseen shift to virtual instruction, principals were not prepared for the demands placed on them either. According to Johnson and Weiner (2020),

> Many principals maintain much of their prior efforts while also meeting the unprecedented challenges the pandemic has created for their staff, families and students. Principals serve as essential, frontline workers, handing out food to families, bringing laptops and tablets to students, keeping up the morale of students through email blasts, parades through students' neighborhoods and continuous messaging and communication to parents. Principals have found new ways to keep cherished school traditions such as prom, graduations and awards ceremonies alive. The focus on doing what is best for kids may never have been more apparent. (p. 367)

Though maintaining morale is certainly important, principals had to also continue to supervise instruction, monitor curriculum, provide professional learning experiences, manage personnel, and so on. All of the traditional leadership expectations, though, had to be performed virtually. This new challenge was not fully realized until the curriculum platform issues were resolved.

Hanna, an experienced high school principal, describes her transition to being a virtual principal:

> All of a sudden, I had to be much more techno-savvy than I ever thought I could possibly be. And learning all of the different programs and things that would be best for my teachers. Trying to find avenues for our career and technical classes that are so hands on . . . and what can I purchase to make the transition easier for them.

Many districts chose the platforms for their schools, and these platforms varied from platforms that provided the curriculum and instruction, such as Edgenuity and Schoology, to platforms that provided the virtual shell within which teachers could build their courses, such as Blackboard and Canvas.

In either scenario, the principal had to become competent to learn all of the platforms needed in order to support teacher and student learning. Then, the principal had to ensure that all teachers received the necessary training on the platforms in order to be successful. Decisions based on platforms should include teacher leadership and include elements such as ease of use, grading options, video size, number of attachments, and so forth.

The next challenge arose when determining how the professional learning was to be provided to teachers. Video conferencing software then had to be explored, such as Google Meets, Zoom, and Microsoft Teams. Of course, principals and teachers had to learn how to navigate video conferences as well. These new conferencing platforms required additional training also. Once all of these issues were settled, though, the tough challenge began with learning to engage students with technology. The impact of disengagement is too large to ignore.

TECHNOLOGY'S IMPACT ON DISADVANTAGED STUDENTS

For children in care, split homes, or low-income households, schools may provide the only constant support in their lives, and without that routine of support, students may turn away from learning (Baker, 2020). In fact, when students are learning away from school, the home environment becomes a critical factor. Parental engagement is a vital component of student success, and administrators have to ensure that all parents are supported through the process.

However, students who benefit more from school-provided structure are less likely to have the home learning environment needed (Montacute, 2020), and parents may not have the time, resources, or skills needed to provide adequate support. As such, these children may be disproportionately impacted by virtual learning (Lee & Morling, 2020). This is not to say that these parents do not want an equitable opportunity for their children; it is just that they do not have the resources or knowledge to support the learners.

For principals, this negative impact on students means that principals have to work overtime to ensure the disadvantaged students are receiving quality, engaging instruction. This overtime effort may include providing technology and resources but it may also indicate a need for a stronger system of follow-through for students with more communication. The *Principal's Corner* below illustrates a case study of the importance of communication in a virtual setting. See Figure 5.1 for a representation of the student support virtual system process.

> *Virtual learning has been complex for the class of 2024, the freshmen class. These students were newly out of middle school and in the middle of Covid-19. In their eighth-grade year, they received 50s for work not turned in and were passed on to Warrior Nation. We began by having Zoom meetings with our students before entering the Freshman Academy with our freshman teachers, behavior management personnel, school counselors, and administration. We discussed with the parents and students the student behavior infractions they may have incurred in the eighth grade and how we could assist them in making*

their freshmen year a successful one. We placed these students on behavior contracts and attendance contracts, getting ready for the fall and their first semester as Warriors.

Fall semester, we began the school year virtually. We had a number of students not completing assignments, so we ran weekly reports. We had our classified staff calling students who did not Zoom with their teachers or turn in assignments. (Yes, we created a script for our staff members.) I spoke with our RTI coordinator and stated that we still needed to go through our processes. We had the teachers complete JotForms that went to our student services team, social worker, school counselors, behavior management specialist, and the grade level administrator. Teachers would complete the JotForm for students who either suffered grades below a 60, missed three days consecutively, or demonstrated behavior concerns. Once the teacher finished the JotForm, the student services team called the parents and set up Zoom conferences with the parents, teachers, school counselors, RTI coordinator, and administrator.

We would then create a plan of action for the student. Options included RTI assistance, after-school tutoring by Zoom, or Saturday school tutoring by Zoom. After setting the plan in place, we would follow up within three weeks to see if the student's grades, attendance, or behavior improved as indicated by the SMART goal we set together.

Now, the other bookend of the grade level was our seniors. Senioritis for some of these seniors set in during Covid-19 and especially in the virtual learning world. They were working jobs at various fast-food restaurants, grocery stores, and Walmart. Some were working these jobs to help support their families when other family members lost jobs.

We scheduled Zoom meetings with our lead school counselor and met with parents and students. Sometimes we could only catch the student driving in the car. Teachers had to be willing to collaborate on a solution for these students. I spoke with our English IV teacher, for example, and we developed a plan for unit recovery for those seniors who were failing.

In one of our Zoom meetings, we caught two of our senior girls in the car together, and we explained the situation that failing English would impact their graduating. We had to make students face the facts that they could either graduate with their peers or during the summer, but they would have to do the work if they wanted to graduate. Both girls stated that they wanted to graduate on June 16. We created their plan to complete unit recovery on Edgenuity. We had to establish midpoint dates to progress monitor their efforts and set a deadline for completion of units. To ensure all information was shared, we Zoom conferenced with their parents, and all agreed to the plan by April 9. These two seniors met their halfway goal and completed the units of recovery for the third quarter.

We follow these processes for grades, attendance, and behaviors at Warrior Nation. The student services team meets every Monday at 2:30 pm to discuss these students' concerns and tweak or refine the processes. We are constantly reflecting on how to support our teachers, and especially our parents and students.

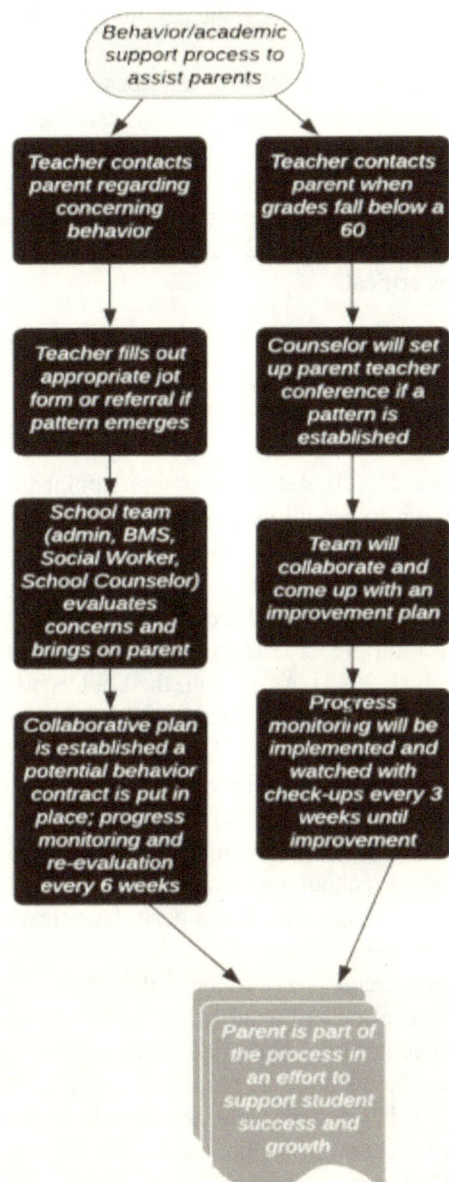

Figure 5.1 Virtual Student Support Model

In the above model, the teacher is initially contacting the parents when there is an initial concern about either behavior or grades. Conferences follow with documentation to support the concerns provided. The third step in both processes involves teacher teams and collaborative planning for supports and interventions. Also included is making the parent part of the process the entire way through.

The principal, in the above scenario, describes adapting her processes to ensure student accountability and support for learning. She also describes teacher collaboration to ensure student success. Warrior Nation, as she describes it, is a high poverty school in which all students receive free lunch. Students' needs to help support their families as well as lack of student engagement in instruction were large obstacles they had to overcome. Communication was critical.

TECHNOLOGY'S IMPACT ON STUDENT ENGAGEMENT

Sonnemann and Goss (2020) stated the obvious point that there is a good reason to send children to school because students learn less when they are not in a regular classroom setting. No doubt, students can be excited by using technology in the classroom. In fact, because of technology, students today have more access to information and ideas (Fitton et al., 2013; Kaye, 2016), and many have had multiple experiences with technology prior to entering school (Hsin, Li, & Tsai, 2014). As a result, the US Department of Education mandated that schools find ways to successfully integrate technology into instruction (King & South, 2017).

Schools have done just that but in varying degrees. Imagine being that child in the classroom with the teacher introducing a fun learning activity or the use of computers to complete an assignment. Students can clearly be motivated by the use of technology because it relates to their world experiences and it is a variance from sitting in a desk, face-forward.

This motivation, however, is also dependent on how the teacher utilizes that technology, as researchers have found that mobile technology is thought to have positive perceptions of student collaboration, but instead found increased disengagement during class time (Heflin, Shewmaker, & Nguyen, 2017). Therefore, teacher technology readiness is a factor in student engagement. With Covid-19, if teachers were not already technology ready, they were thrust into that technology without a choice. An even bigger factor is that motivation with the use of technology dissipates without the teacher's guidance and follow-up.

The key factor during the pandemic is technology was not utilized as an enhancement, but instead it was utilized as the sole source of curriculum, instructional activities, and assessments. Couple that with the fact that students in grades six through twelve suffer more disengagement from school in a normal setting (Brenneman, 2016), and the move to remote learning spelled learning loss for many.

This disengagement has disproportionately impacted students who may have already been falling behind before the pandemic. In fact, these students may have fallen even further behind. Sonnemann and Goss (2020) stated,

> Many disadvantaged students, who were already falling behind before the crisis, will have slipped further back. We find the achievement gap widens at triple the rate in remote schooling compared to regular class. Even if remote learning was working well, disadvantaged students are likely to have learnt at about 50 per cent of their regular rate, losing about a month of learning over a two-month lockdown. (p. 3)

Therefore, the need to ensure teachers are prepared for technology integration is vital. Even though the effects of the Covid-19 pandemic may subside, the virtual Pandora's box has been opened. This box will not close any time soon. Kay, an experienced high school principal, stated, "Technology is a way of life and must be embraced for learning. We can't avoid it any longer. . . . This door is open it is not going away." Therefore, the key for administrators will be anticipating technology needs and emerging technologies in order to better help teachers and students.

Table 5.1 below provides a list of free technologies that support student engagement that can be explored and utilized.

ANTICIPATING TECHNOLOGY NEEDS

Working to understand current technology needs is hard enough but planning for future technology needs seems daunting for many. However, it is not as intimidating as it sounds.

Kay, an experienced high school principal, reinforces this in the following quote:

> [Virtual principals] need to have a sense of what is possible versus being a technology expert. Have a sense of what the technology is available and can do in the instructional environment. . . . It's beyond Principalship 101. I've been doing this for thirty years, so I don't need Principalship 101. We need the things that are timely and useful in the moment. We need people directing professional development programs to look ahead. . . . This use of technology shouldn't have been a surprise. We've been talking about integration of technology into the classroom for two decades now and it has lagged behind the private sector enormously.

Table 5.1 Free Technologies That Support Student Engagement

Application	Purpose	Website
Kami	Writable PDF document for collaborative groups—visible to all	https://www.kamiapp.com
Padlet	Students create virtual sticky notes for brainstorming ideas or answering questions—visible to all	https://padlet.com
Jamboard	Digital whiteboard for collaborative work—visible to all	https://jamboard.google.com
Linoit	Virtual sticky note service to post memos, lists, photos, etc.—visible to all when responding by email	https://en.linoit.com
Canva	Collaborative presentations, videos, Instagram posts, Facebook posts, posters, etc.	https://canva.com
Flipgrid	Collaborative video discussion tool	https://flipgrid.com
Gliffy	Collaborative whiteboard for diagrams	https://gliffy.com
Jeopardy	Play Jeopardy-like games with content	https://jeopardylabs.com
Kahoot!	Class game for content knowledge—can work in teams	https://kahoot.it
Socrative	Games for content knowledge—interactive activities, exit tickets, quizzes	https://www.socrative.com
Mindmeister	Collaborative mind map creation	https://mindmeister.com
Quizziz	Collaborative quizzes and polls or individual	https://quizizz.com
Animoto	Collaborative videos with pictures, music, and speech	https://www.animoto.com
Spark	Collaborative videos, presentations with music, photos, videos, text, and speech	https://spark.adobe.com

With this in mind, principals must stay current of technology trends in education and allow for exploration among staff.

For example, in one large high school, the principal provided professional development on how to use document cameras to engage students in instruction and save instructional time, especially in mathematics and English. After the professional development, the principal asked who among the staff would like a document camera as an instructional tool in the classroom. As a result, the principal purchased document cameras for one hundred teachers at the price of $100 each. Categorical funds were used to purchase these cameras, and teachers had to report on their lesson plans their use.

In a study of over 645 teachers and 90 principals, a direct correlation between a principal's technology leadership and teacher technology integration was found. Additionally, quality professional development on the use of that technology further enhanced the significance of the two variables (Thannimalai & Raman, 2018). Furthermore, another study found that students believe that teacher use of technology is crucial to their performance (Hoffmann & Ramirez, 2018). So how does a principal manage technological growth among all of the other duties assigned?

One way to stay current, again, is to utilize the staff. Many teachers are afraid of technology, but there are others who thrive utilizing new technologies. Therefore, utilizing teacher teams to explore technologies, pilot technologies, and provide professional development on technologies is good practice. Of course, principals must also become proficient in those technologies in order to provide support. In addition, principals should have an expectation of active student engagement while using the technologies. See the following *Principal's Corner* for a real principal experience in making technology decisions.

PROFESSIONAL DEVELOPMENT STRATEGIES

As school systems seek to improve, teachers are constantly attending professional development. In fact, these authors know of no other profession that requires as much professional learning as the teaching profession. To begin, students are not consistent, meaning they come to school with different needs and challenges each year. Pair that with curricula changes as well as technology changes, and continued growth is dictated for all educators to remain successful.

Frankly, teachers need to learn to use technologies in order to better prepare students for the twenty-first-century workforce (Jan, 2017). In addition, this professional learning is critical to any innovative strategy or program that is aimed at improving education for students (Darling-Hammond, 2017; Fullan, 2007). H. Cui and D. Zhang (2018) stated, "The main purpose of teacher professional development is to improve their own quality and lifelong learning ability, keep pace with the times, innovate constantly, improve teaching quality and improve teaching effect" (p. 324).

The *Principal's Corner* below describes technology planning during the pandemic.

> *For most of our technology decisions, the district technology team determines the processes. Still, when we see a software program that our teachers would like to purchase, we take time to analyze how this will work for our students or, better yet, conduct a small PDSA cycle (plan, do, study, and act).*
>
> *The process involves the following steps:*
>
> - *Train a teacher or a group of teachers who are invested in the technology program to implement the program with their students.*

- *Analyze the critical attributes in implementing the program with fidelity.*
- *Plan how you will train your staff by bringing professional development into the building or through the train-the-trainer model.*
- *Tweak the concerns or processes.*
- *Analyze data for students' growth.*
- *Repeat the cycle with the entire staff.*

We recently used Achieve 3000 with our students. I was presented with Reading Plus at an administration meeting for principals. The program looked interesting and may fit our needs for remediation and enrichment. I had the representative come to our school to present to the English teachers. As a small group, we decided we could utilize Reading Plus with our students who are in our foundational and enrichment courses. The teachers who teach these courses will receive the training to learn the software and implement it with fidelity. I tell the staff, we must learn fast to execute well.

So, yes, technology integration and professional development are absolutely necessary. Particular to technology, Christina, a school superintendent with extensive experience, highlights the importance of professional development in this area.

Technology skills. . . . I had to go to a lot of sessions and professional development myself, and I've realized that our teachers need a plethora of professional development, so they feel comfortable teaching virtually.

Teachers are inundated with professional learning, so the challenge is to make the learning meaningful and impactful. In order to do so, Darling-Hammond, Hyler, and Gardner (2017) describe the seven elements of effective professional development as the following:

1. Focuses content—the learning is utilized specific to content areas.
2. Incorporates active learning—teachers engage in the learning and utilize the new tools, calling on their own expertise.
3. Supports collaboration and is job-embedded—teachers can work in groups during the day to practice the learning.
4. Utilizes models/modeling—teachers are shown "how to" incorporate learning.
5. Provides coaching—teachers are provided support to master practices.
6. Sustains duration—learning is not a onetime workshop but offers multiple opportunities to engage in learning around a single practice.

Each of these factors must be considered when designing and planning technology for professional learning. Below in Figure 5.2 is a sample plan for professional learning that includes technology integration.

Thursday Community of Professional Learners (CPL) 2020-2021

Warriors on the Warpath for Excellence!

Date	Week	Outcome	Facilitator
Coaching Cycle 1: SLOs, 4.0 Rubric Intro, & Classroom Management Procedures			
August 31, 2020	1	Classroom Management & Procedures	Dickson/Simmons-Hill/Burvenich
September 1, 2020	2	Orientation SLOs and 4.0 Rubric	Dickson/McGrath
September 10, 2020	3	Reflection on SLOs, Rubric, and Classroom Management & Procedures	Shelia Alston/Lynn Garrett/Admin
Coaching Cycle 2: Instructional Planning and Assessment Mapping			
September 17, 2020	4	Refining SLOs and 4.0	Shelia Alston/Lynn Garrett/Admin
September 24, 2020	6	Diving Deeper Into Google Classroom, Accessing Rubicon & Assessment Mapping with Technology	Estee Williams/Shelia Alston/LynnGarrett
October 1, 2020	7	SLO Share Out and Data Conference Questions	Shelia Alston/Lynn Garrett
October 5-9, 2020	8	Data Conferences and Technology Questions on Thursday	Admin/Estee Williams
October 15, 2020	9	Balancing Formative and Summative Assessment Mapping	Shelia Alston/Lynn Garrett
October 22 2020	10	Standards-Based Assessments with Technology	Estee Williams
October 29, 2020	11	Assessment Mapping Share Out/RTI	Alston/Garrett/Williams
Coaching Cycle 3: Lesson Structure & Pacing with Academic Feedback			
November 5, 2020	12	Gradual Release and Taking Academic Temp with Academic Feedback	Shelia Alston/Lynn Garrett
November 12, 2020	13	Hyperdocs for Structure and Feedback	Estee Williams
November 19, 2020	14	Going Deeper with Gradual Release & Taking Academic Temperature	Shelia Alston/Lynn Garrett
November 26, 2020		Thanksgiving Break	
December 3, 2020	15	Reflection and Analysis of Student Work (Gradual Release)	Shelia Alston/Lynn Garrett
December 10, 2020	16	Google Games for Structure & Feedback	Estee Williams
December 17, 2020	17	Exam Week: Reflect and Grade Completion	WBECHS
December 24, 2020		Winter Break	
January 7, 2020	18	Preparing for Final Data Conferences	Shelia Alston/Lynn Garrett
January 11-15, 2020	19	Data Conferences/Wrapping Up SLOs/Tech RTI on Thursday	Admin/Williams
Coaching Cycle 4: Grouping Students with Meaningful Roles & Sentence Frames			
January 21, 2020	20	Grouping Students with Meaningful Roles & Sentence Frames	Shelia Alston/Lynn Garrett
January 28, 2021	21	Using Technology for Grouping	Estee Williams
February 4, 2021	22	Academic Conversations Within Groups	Shelia Alston/Lynn Garrett

Figure 5.2 Sample technology integration professional development plan

SUMMARY

Principals were not prepared for the shift to virtual leadership, just as students and teachers were not prepared for the shift to virtual learning. Technology preparedness played a critical role for principals, teachers, and students.

Principal struggles rolled down to the student-level and impacted student achievement. As students achieve more when they are in the school environment and have set routines, students in poverty or disadvantaged youth have been impacted more by learning losses during the pandemic. Therefore, principals need to strategically plan technology needs and professional learning needs of teachers as well as virtual student support systems for those falling behind and for future virtual opportunities to ensure student engagement.

Quality professional development requires seven elements to be considered: focused content, active learning, collaboration, modeling, coaching, and duration. Principals can form technology teams in their schools to explore new technologies and pilot them prior to providing professional learning and expending funds.

POLISHING THE DIAMOND

1. What impact did the abrupt shift to virtual education have on principals? Why?
2. What technology needs had to be addressed?
3. Why are disadvantaged youth impacted disproportionately by the switch to virtual education?
4. How can schools respond to this disparity?
5. How has virtual learning impacted student engagement? Why?
6. How can a principal anticipate technology needs?
7. What is a sound method of choosing technology?
8. What factors affect the impact of professional learning?

REFERENCES

Baker, J. (2020, April 12). The kids who will never return to school after COVID-19. *Sydney Morning Herald.* Available from https://www.smh.com.au/national/the-kids-who-will-never-return-toschool-after-covid-19-20200411-p54j0e.html

Brenneman, R. (2016). Gallup student poll finds engagement in school dropping by grade level. *Education Week, 35*(25), 6.

Cui, H., & Zhang, D. (2018). Strategies on teacher professional development in big data era. In *2018 4th International Conference on Education Technology, Management and Humanities Science (ETMHS 2018)* (pp. 324–328). Paris: Atlantis Press.

Darling-Hammond, L. (2017). Teacher education around the world: What can we learn from international practice? *European Journal of Teacher Education, 40*(3), 291–309.

Darling-Hammond, L., Hyler, M. E., & Gardner, M. (2017). *Effective teacher professional development.* Palo Alto, CA: Learning Policy Institute.

Fitton, V. A., Ahmedani, B. K., Harold, R. D., & Shifflet, E. D. (2013). The role of technology on young adolescent development: Implications for policy, research and practice. *Child and Adolescent Social Work Journal, 30*(5), 399–413.

Fullan, M. (2007). *The new meaning of educational change* (4th ed.). New York: Teachers College Press.

Gurley, L. E. (2018). Educators' preparation to teach, perceived teaching presence, and perceived teaching presence behaviors in blended and online learning environments. *Online Learning, 22*(2), 179–220.

Heflin, H., Shewmaker, J., & Nguyen, J. (2017). Impact of mobile technology on student attitudes, engagement, and learning. *Computers & Education, 107,* 91–99.

Hoffmann, M. M., & Ramirez, A. Y. (2018). Students" attitudes toward teacher use of technology in classrooms. *Multicultural Education, 25*(2), 51–56.

Howard, S., Tondeur, J., Siddiz, F., & Sherer, R. (2020). Ready, set, go! Profiling teachers' readiness for online teaching in secondary education. *Technology, Pedagogy, and Education, 30*(1), 137–154.

Hsin, C., Li, M., & Tsai, C. (2014). The influence of young children's use of technology on their learning: A review. *Educational Technology & Society, 17*(4), 85–99.

Jan, H. (2017). Teacher of 21st century: Characteristics and development. *Research on Humanities and Social sciences, 7*(9), 50–54.

Johnson, C., & Weiner, J. (2020). Principal professionalism in the time of COVID-19. *Journal of Professional Capital and Community, 5*(3–43/4), 367–374.

Kaye, L. (Ed.). (2016). *Young children in a digital age: Supporting learning and development with technology in early years.* New York: Routledge.

King, J., & South, J. (2017). *Reimagining the role of technology in higher education: A supplement to the national education technology plan.* Washington, DC: US Department of Education, Office of Educational Technology.

Kniffin, K. M., Narayanan, J., Anseel, F., Antonakis, J., Ashford, S. P., Bakker, A. B., . . . & Vugt, M. V. (2021). COVID-19 and the workplace: Implications, issues, and insights for future research and action. *American Psychologist, 76*(1), 63.

Lee, A., & Morling, J. (2020). Coronavirus disease 2019: Emerging lessons from the pandemic. *Public Health.* doi:10.1016/j.puhe.2020.05.012.

Montacute, R. (2020). *Social mobility and COVID-19: Implications of the COVID-19 crisis for educational inequality.* https://www.suttontrust.com/wp-content/uploads/2020/04/COVID-19-and-Social-Mobility-1.pdf

Sonnemann, J., & Goss, P. (2020). *Covid catch-up: Helping disadvantaged students close the equity gap.* Carlton, Victoria: Grattan Institute.

Thannimalai, R., & Raman, A. (2018). The influence of principals" technology leadership and professional development on teachers" technology integration in secondary schools. *Malaysian Journal of Learning and Instruction, 15*(1), 203–228.

Williamson, B., Eynon, R., & Potter, J. (2020). Pandemic politics, pedagogies and practices: Digital technologies and distance education during the coronavirus emergency. *Learning, Media and Technology, 45*(2), 107–114.

Chapter 6

Leadership Soft Skills

> Soft skills get little respect, but they will make or break your career.
>
> —Peggy Klaus

SOFT SKILLS

Lunenburg (2010) highlights that principals spend the vast majority of their time and effort interacting with others in the learning environment and community. This necessitates soft leadership skills to effectively communicate, motivate, and coordinate a wide range of diverse stakeholder groups, including teachers, professional staff, students, parents, and members of the community (Lunenburg, 2010).

Goodwin (2013) asserts that a principal's success is dependent upon the strength of their people skills or soft leadership skills. Results from research on effective supervision in corporate organizations and educational organizations mirror each other, indicating that soft leadership skills are essential in both environments (Goodwin, 2013).

Goodwin (2013) highlights four key leadership soft skills necessary for effective principal leadership, including effectively coaching others, holding regular meetings with employees, conveying a personal interest in others, and posing insightful questions. Goodwin (2013) argues that the absence of these characteristics leads to high principal turnover rates.

Lunenburg (2010) highlights the expansion of awareness around the importance of strong leadership soft skills in recent years. Lunenburg (2010) states,

> School administrators at all levels need to take care of the human side of the enterprise. Excellent schools and excellent leaders provide warm, nurturing, caring, trusting, and challenging environments. In this view, effective principals are cheerleaders, facilitators, coaches, and nurturers of champions. They build

their organizations through people. Effective human skills enable principals to unleash the energy within staff members and help them grow, ultimately resulting in maximum performance and goal attainment.

The need for soft leadership skills was even more pronounced in the transition to the virtual principalship. In fact, in the mixed-method study, all the interview participants also noted the importance of strong skills in conveying flexibility, empathy, and patience as a key area of virtual principal knowledge, skill, and abilities. This sentiment is described by John, a high school principal with four years of experience, in the following quote,

> The most critical aspect of leaders during this time is keeping the morale and mindset of teachers checked-in. We've had a tremendous focus on supporting our teachers. . . . I have a belief that every teacher is doing the very best they can do every day when they come to school, just like students. Now you could be in a bad place and your best is not the best you've ever done, but it's the best that you've got that day. . . . So keeping up with their emotional status and taking pressure off them.

John adds, "You don't always get it right. The solutions don't always work. But as a leader, 100 percent, they just care that you tried."

During the pandemic, schools did not get it all right. Research predicts both learning losses and a widening of the achievement gap (Dorn et al., 2020; Kuhfeld et al., 2020; Kuhfeld & Tarasawa, 2020). However, what would have happened if principals had not jumped into action with a growth mindset and soft leadership skills to lead a quick transition to virtual instruction? Principals helped salvage the remainder of the school year and used those learning lessons to plan for an even more successful subsequent school year.

FLEXIBILITY

Flexibility skills enable educational leaders to rapidly adapt to change and foster agility in navigating organizations through changing environments. Flexibility can often be critical in remaining productive as a leader during times of great change or challenge. Principals' flexibility is also a key factor in leadership readiness and correctly reading the situational needs and follower readiness of employees within the educational environment (Rajbhandari et al., 2014).

During the transition to the virtual principalship, flexibility was noted by principals as one of the most important leadership elements. Christina, a school superintendent with extensive experience, shares this belief in the following statement:

You've got to be real flexible. . . . You need to have some experience in the brick-and-mortar world. You can't just pick up someone and drop them in a virtual world and say, "Swim."

Donna, a high school principal with three years of experience, states, "You have to be flexible." Similarly, Melanie, a high school principal with extensive experience, shares,

> Learn to be more flexible. . . . I'm listening to [teachers] more. I have to make a conscious effort to listen and be more patient. . . . This has made me look at social and emotional elements for staff.

Principal's Corner

The following *Principal's Corner* describes a scenario where soft leadership skills helped to motivate others. Flexibility is highlighted as a key leadership soft skill that helped signal empathy and build team cohesion. As you read the following scenario, reflect on the importance of practicing what you preach as a leader. There is a tremendous amount of focus on soft skills for graduates entering the workforce and the need to incorporate soft skills in schools. However, it is critical for principals to model it as well.

> *When you talk about soft skills, there are so many: communication, teamwork, problem-solving, time management, critical thinking, decision-making, organizational, stress management, adaptability, conflict management, leadership, creativity, resourcefulness, persuasion, and openness to criticism.*
>
> *In utilizing these skills, you want to build an openness and growth mindset in your building where anyone can approach you with an idea or thought to make the organization run like a well-oiled machine. I showed the soft skills of flexibility, communication, and teamwork when I collaborated with the custodial staff. They were feeling overwhelmed with the Covid-19 protocols and systems, especially during the hybrid cleaning.*
>
> *I listened to their concerns about teachers coming into the building during the deep cleaning. I remember Mag and Tracy telling me, "MLD, how do you expect us to clean while the staff is still in the building? We will not be able to deep clean and sanitize like you want." So we collaborated, and I decided for teachers to work from home on Wednesdays, and the custodians were able to deep clean the building and sanitize with the Halo machine.*
>
> *We created a plan that kept the students and faculty safe while also empowering and motivating them while meeting their needs and valuing their strengths.*

EMPATHY

Empathy is a critically important skill for highly effective educational leaders. Empathy is conveyed through a principal's ability to demonstrate how they relate to other individuals' experiences and emotions. Empathy is far more complex skill than simply expressing sympathy, which requires understanding others and expressing compassion or being sensitive to their needs (Gentry, Weber, & Sadri, 2016). Empathy is a fundamental leadership building block that is the basis of many leadership theories and constructs, including authentic, servant, and transformational leadership (Gentry, Weber, & Sadri, 2016; Walumbwa et al., 2008).

Emotional intelligence, critically important to being an effective leader, also relies on a leader's ability to feel and express empathy (Bar-On & Parker, 2000; George, 2000; Gentry, Weber, & Sadri, 2016). Gentry, Weber, and Sadri (2016) state,

> Leaders now need to lead people, collaborate with others, be able to cross organizational and cultural boundaries and need to create shared direction, alignment, and commitment between social groups with very different histories, perspectives, values, and cultures. It stands to reason that empathy would go a long way toward meeting these people-oriented managerial and leadership requirements.

The importance of empathy as a key leadership component was especially pronounced during the transition to the virtual principalship. Don, an experienced school superintendent, notes, "In the midst of a virtual landscape, this notation of concern and care and support, though different, are still the hallmarks of what is good in education." Similarly, Jack, a first-year principal, shares the following observation: "It's all about adaptability. You have to be patient. You have to have compassion, empathy, and sympathy."

During the Covid-19 pandemic, educators, students and their families, and stakeholders in the community navigated a time of great uncertainty and loss. Some lost family members to the virus, and others experienced economic loss due to business closures, while others navigated sickness or grieved the loss of social interactions and activities they were accustomed to in daily life. Principals had to demonstrate empathy and attend to these feelings and psychological needs in their school communities.

Appreciative inquiry (AI) can enrich how leaders convey empathy and enhance stakeholder engagement, especially during change management, assessment, and evaluation processes. For example, when a program evaluation begins, it may seem appropriate to focus on what is wrong and then develop a plan to fix it. While it certainly is true that an evaluation effort may bring to light weaknesses that need to be addressed, an alternative approach to change management has a track record of positive results. That approach is based on AI, a positive process for organizational change and development.

AI is based on the 4-D Cycle, developed by David Cooperrider and Ronald Fry (Grieten et al., 2018). The 4-D Cycle comprises the following four elements (Grieten et al., 2018).

- **Discovery**—employees are asked to identify and explore the organization's key strengths.
- **Dream**—employees are asked to dream about the future accomplishments they would like to see the organization achieve.
- **Design**—employees are asked to leverage best practices and strengths identified during the discovery phase and design strategies toward accomplishing the dream goals.
- **Destiny**—employees implement strategies and engage in continuous improvement efforts toward the dream accomplishments.

Principals can use the core tenets of AI to help create stronger team unity and engagement in the planning process. It can also be powerful in modeling and fostering a growth mindset. For example, prompting employees to reflect on the school's strengths and envision what they would like to see the organization accomplish in the future can help focus the learning community on next steps and foster forward progress.

PATIENCE

Patience is a powerful leadership skill and can help leaders ensure meaningful and enduring changes within educational environments. In times of significant change or challenge, patience can be undervalued as a skill in lieu of quick, decisive decisions. However, patience can help leaders ensure they are acting with purpose, persistence, and endurance to stay the course that will best benefit their organizations and stakeholders in the end (Eich, 2015, 2017).

In his book, *Truth, Trust + Tenacity: How Ordinary People Become Extraordinary Leaders*, Ritch Eich (2015) describes key characteristics of great leaders throughout the world. He argues that in addition to an important component of leadership, patience can also be seen as an acronym for a grouping of valuable leadership characteristics. Eich (2015) states,

> If you look at the characteristics of some of the world's greatest leaders, you may notice what I did: purpose, approachability, tolerance, independence,

empathy, nurturing nature, confidence, and endurance. It's not a coincidence that these words make up the acronym patience.

This quote is illustrative of the experience of virtual principals during the Covid-19 pandemic, who practiced patience to ensure they met the needs of teachers and staff, students, and the community. Virtual principals also modeled patience as a key skill for others throughout the educational environment. For example, principals viewed trial and error with technologies as part of the learning process and provided professional development resources for learning more about technology best practices.

For those who don't have an incredible amount of patience, there are key steps that can help further develop this leadership soft skill. Building in the time for reflection and considering the feelings of others can help convey patience to stakeholders. Practice and awareness are also helpful strategies that can be exercised through engagement in professional development.

PROFESSIONAL DEVELOPMENT STRATEGIES

While some leaders naturally project empathy, flexibility, and patience, many other leaders find themselves somewhere in the middle of the soft skills continuum. Viewing these skills through a growth mindset is critically important, as these skills can be learned and refined through professional development, coaching, and training (Dweck, 2006; Gentry, Weber, & Sadri, 2016; Ricci, 2018). Gentry, Weber, and Sadri (2016) suggest there are five key ways in which organizations can aid leaders in developing and strengthening their leadership soft skills.

1. **Communicate about the importance of empathy.** Educate leaders about why understanding, caring, and investing in the development of others is important in the educational environment as well as how it enhances their own effectiveness.
2. **Provide listening skills training.** Leaders can better understand others and sense emotions within the learning community if they actively listen as well as listen to hear both verbal and nonverbal messages.
3. **Encourage and practice perspective taking.** Professional development activities and exercises that encourage reflection based upon putting oneself in others' shoes can be helpful in gaining insights and deeper understanding of the experiences of employees.
4. **Focus on cultivating compassion.** Encouraging opportunities to consider the feelings of others and the effects of leadership decisions on employees, students, and communities is critically important. Creating

time for reflection and compassionate response can help cultivate empathy, flexibility, and patience.
5. **Professional development on working across cultures.** Working across cultures enables leaders to strengthen their understanding of and appreciation for different perspectives and experiences.

Districts can invest in principal professional development, coaching, and networking activities that address these five important areas. Practice is critical in sharpening one's leadership soft skills. Utilizing case studies and mock employee performance coaching sessions can provide valuable practice within a professional development environment.

SUMMARY

This chapter explores the role of leadership soft skills in effective virtual principalship. Strong skills in conveying flexibility, empathy, and patience are especially important in virtual leadership and fostering positive organizational morale. Best practices, strategies, and professional development activities for strengthening the ability to communicate flexibility, empathy, and patience in the virtual environment are examined.

POLISHING THE DIAMOND

1. Describe leadership soft skills.
2. Why are leadership soft skills important?
3. What strategies can principals utilize to convey flexibility?
4. What strategies can principals utilize to convey empathy?
5. What strategies can principals utilize to convey patience?
6. What is appreciative inquiry?
7. Describe how principals can use appreciative inquiry to communicate flexibility, empathy, and patience in the learning environment?
8. List three professional development strategies for enhancing principals' leadership soft skills.
9. How can districts support principals in fostering their leadership soft skills? List two ways.

REFERENCES

Bar-On, R., & Parker, J. D. (2000). *The Handbook of Emotional Intelligence.* San Francisco: Jossey-Bass.

Dorn, E., Hancock, B., Sarakatsannis, J., & Viruleg, E. (2020). *COVID-19 and Student Learning in the United States: The Hurt Could Last a Lifetime.* Retrieved https://www.apucis.com/frontend-assets/porto/initial-reports/COVID-19-and-student-learning-in-the-United-States-FINAL.pdf.pagespeed.ce.VHbS948yF4.pdf

Dweck, C. (2006). *Mindset: The New Psychology of Success.* New York: Random House.

Eich, R. (2015). *Truth, Trust + Tenacity: How Ordinary People Become Extraordinary Leaders.* Madison, WI: Second City Publishing.

Eich, R. (2017). On patience in leadership. *The Journal of Values-Based Leadership*, 10(1). Accessed http://dx.doi.org/10.22543/0733.101.1178

Gentry, W. A., Weber, T. J., & Sadri, G. (2016). *Empathy in the Workplace: A Tool for Effective Leadership. The Center for Creative Leadership.* Accessed http://cclinnovation.org/wp-content/uploads/2020/03/empathyintheworkplace.pdf

George, J. M. (2000). Emotions and leadership: The role of emotional intelligence. *Human Relations*, 53, 1027–1055.

Goodwin, B. (2013). Research says a principal's success requires people skills. *The Principalship*, 70(7), 79–80.

Grieten, S., Lambrechts, F., Bouwen, R., Huybrechts, J., Fry, R., & Cooperrider, D. (2018). Inquiring into appreciative inquiry: A conversation with David Cooperrider and Ronald Fry. *Journal of Management Inquiry*, 27(1), 101–114.

Kreitner, R., & Kinicki, A. (2010). *Organizational Behavior* (9th ed.). New York: McGraw-Hill.

Kuhfeld, M., Soland, J., Tarasawa, B., Johnson, A., Ruzek, E., & Liu, J. (2020). Projecting the potential impact of COVID-19 school closures on academic achievement. *Educational Researcher*, 49(8), 549–565.

Kuhfeld, M., & Tarasawa, B. (2020). *The COVID-19 Slide: What Summer Learning Loss Can Tell Us about the Potential Impact of School Closures on Student Academic Achievement.* NWEA. Accessed https://www.nwea.org/content/uploads/2020/05/Collaborative-Brief_Covid19-Slide-APR20.pdf

Lunenburg, F. C. (2010). Communication: The process, barriers, and improving effectiveness. *Schooling*, 1(1), 1–10.

Lunenburg, F. C., & Irby, B. J. (2006). *The Principalship: Vision to Action.* Belmont, CA: Wadsworth/Cengage.

Lunenburg, F. C., & Ornstein, A. O. (2008). *Educational Administration: Concepts and Practices* (5th ed.). Belmont, CA: Wadsworth/Cengage.

Luthans, F. (2011). *Organizational Behavior* (12th ed.). New York: McGraw-Hill.

Rajbhandari, M., Loock, C., Du Plessis, P., & Rajbhandari, S. (2014). *Leadership Readiness for Flexibility and Mobility: The 4th Dimensions on Situational Leadership Styles in Educational* Settings. ERIC Clearinghouse. Accessed https://files.eric.ed.gov/fulltext/ED552915.pdf

Ricci, M. C. (2018). *Create a Growth Mindset School: An Administrator's Guide to Leading a Growth Mindset Community.* Waco, TX: Prufrock Press.

Walumbwa, F. O., Avolio, B. J., Gardner, W. L., Wernsing, T. S., & Peterson, S. J. (2008). Authentic leadership: Development and validation of a theory-based measure. *Journal of Management,* 34, 89–126.

Chapter 7

Instructional Leadership

> Remember diamonds are created under pressure so hold on, it will be your time to shine soon.
>
> —Sope Agbelusi

When teachers know what is expected of them and are provided with proper guidance, support, and resources, they can operate without fear. Most teachers' specific asset to a school is their content knowledge (Hoy, Davis, & Pape, 2006), and this is their strength. However, teachers do not always feel confident in their teaching, which is different from their knowledge (Lewis, 2009; Tygret, 2018). Covid left many teachers feeling insecure and less confident due to the fear of the ineffectiveness of online learning.

So how did administrators fare during Covid in providing that instructional supervisory support? Unfortunately, not as well as they would have liked. In a study, conducted by the authors of this book, South Carolina principals cited virtual instructional leadership as the number one professional development needed during the pandemic. The need for this professional development highlights the need for instructional leadership skills outside of the pandemic, honestly.

What constitutes instructional supervision, one may ask? According to Gulcan (2012), "The basic starting point of instructional leadership is to develop instruction" (p. 626). Additionally, Horng and Loeb (2010) provide a different view of instructional supervision that "emphasizes organizational management for instructional improvement rather than day-to-day teaching and learning" (p. 66). These authors posit it is a combination of the two views that has the greatest impact. More about systems will be covered in the next chapter.

ELEMENTS

There are several elements to consider in virtual instructional supervision, and they must be intentionally defined for teachers and administrators:

1. Curricular alignment and pacing
2. Lesson plan review and feedback
3. Observation and feedback
4. Professional learning communities and feedback
5. Professional development and coaching

John, a high school principal with four years of experience, stated,

> Develop a sound leadership team with teachers and coaches or whoever your instructional supports are, collect data on your school, and respond to the unique challenges that your school faces. Communicat[e] that consistently in every faculty meeting talking about the goals we are accomplishing together.... [M]y learning in the school improvement team process is the sustainability of that and developing teacher leadership to see larger school goals be accomplished.

Curricular Alignment and Pacing

Most school districts provide curriculum guides for teachers that map out state standards. However, curriculum alignment takes the measure a step further and ensures that resources used also align to the standards. If districts do not provide these planners for teachers, then principals must start at this point for teachers. Teachers are more effective when they know what they are supposed to teach in what timeframes, as this shows the connectivity of standards. Additionally, teachers are more apt to stay on target rather than stray into other areas of interest and completely leave standards untouched.

Lesson Plans

Lesson plans play a vital role in instruction that is often overlooked. Lesson plans not only provide a roadmap of instruction for teachers, but also provide a roadmap of learning for administrators (Westberry, 2020). Chizhik and Chizhik (2018) stated that teacher education programs must improve in developing skills of aligning lesson plans with assessment data to focus attention on students' learning needs. Is it that teacher education programs are at fault, or is that administrators do not require lesson plan submission?

The major arguments about lesson plan submissions are the following:

1. Nobody reads them, and no one likes an exercise in futility.
2. Lesson plans take too much time for teachers and create an undo burden when teachers' plates are already full enough.

Let's work from these two issues. First, teachers are correct. Who wants to take the time to create lesson plans if no one is going to read them? Administrators must value the teachers' efforts by reading and providing timely feedback to lesson plans. John Hattie's work, which primarily focuses on student learning, can be applied here. Hattie and Clarke (2019) state the following:

> Feedback is information about the task that fills a gap between what is understood and what is aimed to be understood. It can lead to increased effort, motivation, or engagement to reduce the discrepancy between the current status and the goal; it can indicate that more information is available or needed; it can point to directions that the students could pursue; and it can lead to restructuring understanding. (p. 3)

Teachers need feedback just as much as students do. The feedback just needs to be specific and actionable in order to create a culture of growth (Ford et al., 2017; Liu et al., 2019).

Therefore, lesson plan formatting and required elements need to be clear for teachers so that they can meet the instructional planning expectation. Not to mention, those reading the lesson plans need to be knowledgeable enough about content standards, instructionally aligned pedagogy, and assessments in order to provide valuable feedback.

The importance of lesson plans goes beyond administrator ability to understand what is happening in the classrooms, and this fact cannot be ignored. Research shows that students prefer academic classes if the classes are based on well-planned lesson plans because the activities flow smoothly, instruction is differentiated, and timely feedback is given.

If administrators read lesson plans, then administrators can gather valuable data on the following:

1. Curriculum pacing
2. Curriculum alignment
3. Instructional alignment
4. Assessment alignment

Of course, the last element, assessment alignment, dictates assessments are included with lesson plans that are electronically submitted weekly.

The combination of information allows administrators to quantify data on how a staff is performing, and this will highlight strengths and areas of needed growth. This data then serves to inform professional development needs as well as experts in the building who can help provide that professional development. See Figure 7.1 for a sample virtual lesson plan template.

Administrators have to decide when lesson plans are submitted, to whom, and what the timeframe is for feedback to be given. Preferably, submission

Pre-Assessment Data Delete or add classes and courses as needed.		
Class/Course/Period	Class/Course/Period	Class/Course/Period

	Monday	Tuesday	Wednesday	Thursday	Friday
Standards:					
OBJECTIVES: List the learning targets covered during this lesson.	Students will be able to:	Students will be able to:	Students will be able to:	Students will be able to:	Students will be able to:
Key Resources: Links to sites, documents and other materials used in this lesson.					
Gradual Release: I do We do You do Include links to sites, documents, materials used in this lesson, as well as virtual interactions (chat, poll questions, etc.)					
Assessment: How will you assess learning?					
Exit Ticket:					

Unit Title:					
Assessment Name	Assessment Type (e.g., quiz, homework, Kahoot, exit ticket)	When (e.g. daily, after lesson 2, date, etc.)	Graded (G)/Ungraded (U)	Formative (F) or Summative (S)	Standards Assessed:

Figure 7.1 Virtual lesson plan template

and feedback tasks are completed prior to the teaching of the materials. This gives teachers time to reflect on the feedback and make adjustments, if necessary.

Additionally, administrators need to determine who will read the lesson plans and provide the feedback. One suggestion is to divide the departments, grade levels, and so forth, by leadership team to make the work more manageable. However, all information should be shared among the team.

Observations

Along with lesson plans, administrators should conduct virtual observations regularly. That is, observations are another tool for affirmation and growth, if used properly. Combining lesson plan review along with observations paints a clearer picture. Are teachers really using the instructional strategies that meet the students' needs? Is the lesson actively engaging? How does the teacher use questioning to enhance learning? All can be measured during observations.

Observation Data

There are two types of data to be gleaned from virtual observations: quantitative and qualitative.

Quantitative Data

Quantitative data can be collected when performing virtual walkthrough observations. Even though these walkthroughs only provide a snapshot of information, if the entire leadership team is focused on the same lesson elements, those snapshots can be very informational. Walkthrough observations on their own do not provide enough information to act upon.

A focus for the virtual walkthrough observations should be provided for a specified period of time. Then, all administrators are looking for the same elements in classrooms, and teachers are aware of that fact in advance. For example, one week's focus may be on higher order questioning while the next week's focus may be on student engagement. The foci should reflect the leadership's priorities.

By providing these priorities to teachers, again, they can clearly understand the instructional expectations. The tabulations of virtual walkthrough data collected serve as valuable information for professional development. For example, one week's data may show that ten of fifty-five teachers incorporated higher order thinking, whereas the remaining teachers were utilizing rote questioning in the classrooms. This type of data reveals patterns, and patterns highlight where work is needed. See Table 7.1 below for a quantifiable observation chart.

VIRTUAL WALKTHROUGH OBSERVATION DATA, SEPTEMBER 6–SEPTEMBER 22

Based on the above chart, an administrator may discuss with the leadership team that teachers are not utilizing examples to introduce new material and are not providing feedback in order to monitor and adjust instruction as one would like. Therefore, this data may be shared with the entire faculty, which explains the need for professional development. Also, sharing data in this regard certainly is less threatening because it constitutes "we" need to work on this, rather than "you" need to work on this.

Qualitative Data

Qualitative observation data is more time consuming to obtain, but it still highlights strengths and weaknesses in a building. These virtual observations should last at least twenty to thirty minutes if not a full class period. In this scenario, the observer is scripting the observation so that the observer can notate the demonstration of the focus of the period. Collective data on these observations can help to determine teacher goals, professional development, and any additional teacher supports needed (Westberry, 2020).

Again, best practices can be identified in these observations, which helps to identify teachers who can lead the professional development needed by others. Teachers appreciate professional development led by their peers, and the teachers leading the professional development feel valued for their specific assets. Additionally, this tapping of teachers supports shared leadership and building capacity in the school building (Boylan, 2016; Ghamrawi, 2013). This is a win-win situation for all concerned.

Table 7.1 Sample Quantifiable Observation Data Chart

Focus	# of Observations	Needs
Explicit examples and illustrations utilized for new concepts	18	8
Teacher models performance expectations	17	5
Technology that enhances student learning is incorporated	12	4
Feedback is frequently given and used to monitor and adjust instruction	18	12

Professional Learning Communities

Teachers should continue the work of professional learning communities (PLCs), even in the virtual environment. In fact, teachers have reported more focus in virtual PLCs and less straying from the work to be done. Additionally, teachers, though they prefer face-to-face interactions, still feel that virtual PLCs are effective (McConnell et al., 2013). However, administrators must provide a focus for the work to be done.

The characteristics of PLCs, according to DuFour and Eaker (1998), include a shared vision of learning and a shared inquiry about teaching practices that impact student learning. In fact, properly run PLCs allow teachers to become transformational leaders in their own rights, where transformational leadership is defined as allowing employees to solve problems and increase productivity through collective thought and creativity (Bass & Riggio, 2006).

Administrative focus for PLC meetings also helps to define instructional expectations. The focus can alternate and change, depending on the needs of the school. Sample PLC foci include the following:

1. Lesson development
2. Assessment building
3. Data meetings using assessment data
4. Output examination

Each of these foci are important to consider. Lesson development PLCs work to align instructional strategies to the cognitive level of the standards to be taught. Assessment building PLCs, similarly, ensure the cognitive alignment of the assessment to the standards. Data PLCs examine assessment data to determine which standards were taught well and understood versus those that may need to be retaught.

The final foci presented is often an overlooked one. Output examination PLCs actually examine student work, such as writing and projects, to determine if the lessons garnered the desired output. Did students perform at the level expected?

Teachers, when given a focus for their meetings and proper training, "will exceed expectations and their self-efficacy will greatly expand. Teacher leaders are developed through PLC practice, and those same skills can be applied to other leadership structures such as a school's leadership team" (Westberry, 2020, p. 130). Therefore, administrators should decide their priorities and provide the proper focus and forms for reporting.

In order for principals to understand the progress of a PLC, PLC feedback forms need to be provided so that they can be read and commented upon. Yes, feedback here is critical as well. It is impossible for administrators to attend all PLCs, especially in a large school. Therefore, PLC virtual reporting forms help to inform the principal of the work being done in the school. These forms can also provide an avenue for teachers to ask for assistance as well as provide quantifiable data for administrators to determine professional development needs. See Figure 7.2 for a sample PLC virtual feedback form.

Professional Development

Teacher professional development (PD) is fundamental to improvement (Darling-Hammond, 2017; Sancar, Atal, & Deryakulu, 2021), and Covid-19 provided a larger need for improvement in the online world. Online PD can provide both synchronous and asynchronous support, allowing teachers time to reflect and practice what is learned either individually or in collaboration with PLCs (Hartshorne et al., 2020).

With the addition of virtual PD, administrators can provide more personalized PD. Prior publications note the different cycles of PD: all-teacher PD, new-teacher PD, focused PD for a specific group of teachers or content area, and PLCs (Westberry, 2020). Well, virtual PD even opens the door to more coaching possibilities. Let's put these cycles in perspective.

All-teacher PD is needed when patterns emerge among the faculty, as discussed earlier. Maybe only 20 percent of faculty utilized higher order questioning in classes during a month period; therefore, the faculty may participate in some PD on just that. Administrators will then look for these elements in lesson plans as well as in observations to determine change.

New-teacher PD is designed for new teachers to catch up to the instructional priorities previously established. New teachers are hired every year, but seldom do these teachers get the benefit of training that the rest of the staff

PLC Feedback Form	Subject/Grade Level_____ Date_____
	Focus of PLC:
	Work Completed:
	Findings:
	I need help with the following:

Figure 7.2 Sample PLC virtual feedback form

already experienced. That is why new teachers need their own cycle of PD in addition to the all-teacher PD offered to the entire school.

Focused PD may be department specific, such as mathematics teachers working to understand how to incorporate one of the eight mathematical practices, such as modeling with mathematics. Another area of focused PD may be for a group of teachers who are struggling with an element of the teacher evaluation, such as differentiation of instruction. Yet another application may be to work with teachers who teach English-as-a-second-language students in order to provide them with strategies to develop language acquisition.

The point is that focused PD may touch more than one group of teachers, but the results are the same. Teachers receive the support they need in small groups with others who share the same need. This is less threatening for teachers to collaborate using newly acquired skills. However, this is where coaching comes in. The follow-up of this focused PD may be PLCs. If teachers are provided a focus for the PLC meetings, as previously noted, then the collaborative effort of the PLC may assist with providing additional PD on the topic.

So why is this so difficult for principals? Christina, a school superintendent with extensive experience, asserts that virtual principals must be "more deliberate and more thoughtful about the needs of our teachers, what type of professional development they need, their learning, and what experiences they need."

Professional development should not be considered unless you have the data to support the need. Data from lesson plans, observations, and PLC forms must be collected and analyzed. In a recent study, researchers reported that principals did not adequately support teacher professional development needs such as determining group and individual needs, providing that professional development through resources inside or outside of the school or providing enough reading and research tasks to foster growth (Karacabey, 2020). Maybe principals do not have the needed data to support the efforts.

In either case, PD can be provided virtually asynchronously through video or synchronously via video conferencing, and teachers seem to like this method because they engage with the PD at a more convenient time. In fact, a study of student teachers who were impacted due to Covid-19 found that student teachers who continued learning through an online environment versus the standard environment actually performed better their first year of teaching, according to teacher evaluations (Goldhaber & Ronfeldt, 2020).

Coaching

Affinito (2018) pointed out that virtual coaching coupled with online PD can provide a customizable learning experience that directly impacts teacher practice. The logical next step to ensure successful implementation of strategies or initiative is coaching. The PD is provided virtually, teachers follow up in PLCs for implementation collaboration, and coaching ensues with those who still experience some difficulty. It is the logical next step in the PD world.

Kay, an experienced high school principal, stated,

> The coaching model became more integral when we were completely online. Being there for teachers with words of encouragement and the expertise to say have you tried this . . . have you tried that, and even more importantly, talk to this person. . . . It was important for me to have a really good handle on who among my faculty and staff had this down, who were the go-to people, as well as who is my best building site technology guru in terms of software and hardware systems. Directing them to connect and making those connections come together for people so that everyone's comfort level did increase over the course of the online learning experience. . . . Recognizing that you really do have two very different sets of learners with different needs and this is far beyond classroom differentiation. The physical barriers are extraordinary and how you coach and encourage teachers through that as well as coaching and encouraging students through this transition.

Coaching has been proven to be an effective tool to improve teacher practices (Cohen et al., 2020; Killion, Bryan, & Clifton, 2020; Reddy, Shernoff, & Lekwa, 2021). Virtual coaching is not a new concept and has been found to be just as effective (Rock et al., 2011). No matter the coaching method used, there are at least three stages of the coaching cycle: preobservation conference, classroom observation, and postobservation conference (Hui et al., 2020). However, the style of coaching is important for an administrator to consider.

Coaching teachers in a group or in front of peers may not get the same response as whisper coaching, simply because teachers may feel threatened if recommendations are made in front of others. Whisper coaching occurs when an administrator or instructional coach "whispers" in the ear of the teacher recommendations either as the teacher is teaching or immediately thereafter. Whisper coaching can be very effective in the virtual environment because it can be real-time without disruptions.

In either case, coaching practices must include five elements:

1. Concern for consciousness—Coaching generates the sense of self in awareness, knowledge, and personal monitoring.
2. Concern for connection—Coaches will be more effective with true personal connections with those being coached.

3. Concern for competence—Coaches recognize the current level of competence of the teacher and work to set learning goals together as they build on teacher strengths.
4. Concern for contribution—Coaches help teachers remember their passion for helping children.
5. Concern for creativity—Coaches create a no-fault playground for teachers to feel free to be creative and take the next steps to achieve their goals. (Tschannen-Moran & Tschannen-Moran, 2011)

Consider the following *Principal's Corner* on coaching.

As an administrative team, we meet every Monday morning to discuss our goals, observations, professional development, testing, and athletics for the week and the following week to ensure we are all on the same page. With observations, we discuss the focus for the week. Also, we analyze our notes to see if any of our teachers from the previous week need whisper coaching, modeling, or one-on-one. Our instructional coaches reflect and take notes to work with those teachers who have an area of refinement in the focus area.

This particular week, we discussed transitions in having a definite beginning, middle, and ending in a lesson, lesson structure, and pacing, LSP.

This one teacher was losing instructional time in her transitions. We preconferenced with her and asked her, How are you transitioning from your warm-up or lesson starters, and how long do you usually have them go? We get her to reflect on her practices with LSP and ask her what strategies she could utilize to ensure she is not losing valuable instructional time. We then schedule a time for her to go with us in Zoom during her planning time to see one of our best teachers applying LSP. As we are on Zoom, we email her about noticing specific strategies the teacher uses to ensure no loss in instructional time.

After watching the teacher for thirty minutes, we then get on Zoom to reflect further on what she observed and how she can adapt the strategy she saw within the next class or lesson. During our Zoom, we scheduled a time for either the coach or me to come back to her Zoom to see the strategy in action and give immediate feedback using our Observation Google Form. A postobservation conference is scheduled to discuss the feedback.

Of course, another observation is scheduled with the struggling teacher to see her implement the new strategies, and the teacher received feedback on the observation. This is a perfect whisper coaching cycle, where the teacher who needs further development gets to observe best practices, discuss those practices and how she can implement them in her classroom, and practice the skill learned. The whole process started, however, with administration discussing observation data. In this way, PD can be very personalized virtually. Perhaps principals need that personalization as well.

SUMMARY

Instructional leadership encompasses not only the organization management of learning but also several key elements: lesson plans, observations, professional learning communities, and professional development to include coaching.

Lesson plans provide teachers a roadmap for instruction as they provide administrators a roadmap for learning in their building. Teachers must submit lesson plans and administrators must provide feedback. Quantitative data should be collected from lesson plans in order to establish patterns of strength and areas of growth.

Observations should also provide quantitative and qualitative data for administrators to make informed decisions about professional development. Observations should be focused, and the data should be shared with the school.

Data from lesson plans and observations should be shared with all teachers as a basis for work in PLCs. PLCs should be given a focus: lesson planning, assessment building, data analyses, or output analyses. PLCs should also be given a reporting form, which is submitted to administration, and administrators should provide feedback. These PLC forms also serve as a data point that provides a basis for professional development.

Cycles of professional development should be considered, whether the PD is for all teachers, new teachers, or a focused group of teachers. Professional development should continue in the virtual realm, and that PD can be personalized to the teachers' needs.

One form of personalized PD is coaching. Whisper coaching is very effective because teachers don't feel threatened or embarrassed in front of others. The coaching cycle must be completed despite the type of coaching employed.

All of these elements must work together in an organization that supports the work in order to provide effective instructional supervision in a virtual environment.

POLISHING THE DIAMOND

1. What are four elements of instructional supervision?
2. How can each element be included in the virtual environment?
3. How can you quantify lesson plan data?
4. How can you quantify observation data?
5. What are the four foci of PLCs?

6. What data should be used to inform PD?
7. What are the three cycles of PD every administrator should include in plans?
8. What are the five concerns in coaching?
9. Why is whisper coaching an effective practice?
10. How can you whisper coach in a virtual environment?

REFERENCES

Affinito, S. (2018). *Literacy coaching: Transforming teaching and learning with digital tools and technology*. Portsmouth, NH: Heinemann.

Bass, B., & Riggio, R. (2006). *Transformational leadership*. Mahwah, NJ: Earlbaum Associates Publishing.

Boylan, M. (2016). Enabling adaptive system leadership: Teachers leading professional development. *Educational Management Administration & Leadership, 46*(1), 86–106.

Chizhik, E., & Chizhik, A. (2018). Using activity theory to examine how teachers' lesson plans meet students' learning needs. *The Teacher Educator, 53*(1), 67–85.

Cohen, J., Wong, V., Krishnamachari, A., & Berlin, R. (2020). Teacher coaching in a simulated environment. *Educational Evaluation and Policy Analysis, 42*(2), 208–231.

Darling-Hammond, L. (2017). Teacher education around the world: What can we learn from international practice? *European Journal of Teacher Education, 40*(3), 291–309.

DuFour, R., & Eaker, R. (1998). Professional communities at cork: Best practices for enhancing student achievement. Bloomington, IN: Solution Tree Press.

Ford, T., Van Sickle, M., Clark, L., Fazio-Brunson, M., & Schween, D. (2017). Teacher self-efficacy, professional commitment, and high-stakes teacher evaluation policy in Louisiana. *Education Policy, 31*(2), 202–248.

Ghamrawi, N. (2013). Teachers helping teachers: A professional development model that promotes teacher leadership. *International Education Studies, 6*(4), 171–182.

Goldhaber, D., & Ronfeldt, M. (2020). *Sustaining teacher training in a shifting environment. Brief no. 7.* EdResearch for Recovery Project. ERIC number ED607712.

Gulcan, M. (2012). Research on instructional leadership competencies of school principals. *Education, 132*(3), 625–635.

Hartshorne, R., Baumgartner, E., Kaplan-Rakowski, R., Mouza, C., & Ferdig, R. E. (2020). Special issue editorial: Preservice and inservice professional development during the COVID-19 pandemic. *Journal of Technology and Teacher Education, 28*(2), 137–147.

Hattie, J., & Clarke, S. (2019). *Visible learning: Feedback*. New York: Routledge.

Hong, J. C., Lee, Y. F., & Ye, J. H. (2021). Procrastination predicts online self-regulated learning and online learning ineffectiveness during the coronavirus lockdown. *Personality and Individual Differences, 174*, 110673.

Horng, E., & Loeb, S. (2010). New thinking about instructional leadership. *Phi Delta Kappan, 92*(3), 66–69.

Hoy, A. W., Davis, H., & Pape, S. J. (2006). Teacher knowledge and beliefs. In P. A. Alexander & P. H. Winne (Eds.), *Handbook of educational psychology* (2nd ed., pp. 715–737). Mahwah, NJ: Lawrence Erlbaum.

Hui, K. S., Khemanuwong, T., & Ismail, S. A. M. M. (2020). Keeping teachers afloat with instructional coaching: Coaching structure and implementation. *The Qualitative Report, 25*(7), 1790–1816.

Karacabey, M. F. (2021). School principal support in teacher professional development. *International Journal of Educational Leadership and Management, 9*(1), 54–75.

Killion, J., Bryan, C., & Clifton, H. (2020). Coaching matters. *Learning Forward*. Retrieved https://learningforward.org/coachingmatters/

Lewis, C. (2009). What is the nature of knowledge development in lesson study? *Educational Action Research, 17*(1), 95–110.

Liu, Y., Visone, J., Mongillo, M., & Lisi, P. (2019). What matters to teachers if evaluation is meant to help them improve? *Studies in Educational Evaluation, 61,* 41–54.

McConnell, T. J., Parker, J. M., Eberhardt, J., Koehler, M. J., & Lundeberg, M. A. (2013). Virtual professional learning communities: Teachers' perceptions of virtual versus face-to-face professional development. *Journal of Science Education and Technology, 22*(3), 267–277.

Reddy, L. A., Shernoff, E., & Lekwa, A. (2021). A randomized controlled trial of instructional coaching in high-poverty urban schools: Examining teacher practices and student outcomes. *Journal of School Psychology, 86,* 151–168.

Rock, M., Zigmond, N., Gregg, M., & Gable, R. (2011). The power of virtual coaching. *Educational Leadership, 68*(2), 42–48.

Sancar, R., Atal, D., & Deryakulu, D. (2021). A new framework for teachers' professional development. *Teaching and Teacher Education, 101,* 103305.

Tschannen-Moran, B., & Tschannen-Moran, M. (2011). The coach and the evaluator. *Educational Leadership, 69*(2), 10–16.

Tygret, J. A. (2018). The preparation and education of first-year teachers: A case study. *The Qualitative Report, 23*(3), 710–729. Retrieved from https://nsuworks.nova.edu/tqr/vol23/iss3/15

Westberry, L. (2020). *Putting the pieces together: A systems approach to school leadership*. Lanham, MD: Rowman and Littlefield.

Chapter 8

Systems Approaches

> A diamond doesn't start out polished and shining. It once was nothing special, but with enough pressure and time, becomes spectacular. I'm that diamond.
>
> —Solange Nicole

SYSTEMS

Schools constitute large organizations with many people and moving parts, wherein one decision addressed in one part of the organization may impact another part of the organization. Systems thinking focuses on the whole and how each part affects the others, rather than just focusing on one part at a time (Shaked & Schechter, 2020). School administrators are often caught in the mode of putting out fires, and without a systems approach, the real work of schools can be left undone (Westberry, 2020).

Systems thinking is thought to be an effective way to manage organizations, such as schools, since schools are complex organizations that involve processes in organization, socialization, and learning (Cabrera & Cabrera, 2019). In addition to management functions, systems thinking also supports collaboration and shared decision making (Amsler & O'Leary, 2017; Jaaron & Backhouse, 2014) as well as organizational resilience (Randle & Stroink, 2018). So it is important to understand the systems that exist within a school as well as those lacking.

There are four major systems within a school: a system of curriculum and instruction, a teacher support system, a student support system, and a system of culture (Westberry, 2020). Each of these systems has an impact on the others, which most assuredly impacts student learning. Therefore, it is important to examine all four systems within your school and consider how those systems fared in the virtual environment. Did principals digress to the "putting out fires" mode of operation? Did the systems clearly exist prior to the pandemic?

Melanie, a high school principal with extensive experience, describes her transition to virtual leadership as the following:

> The first thing I did was reflect on what we could still do virtually. . . . We had to look at the current systems we had in place to see what we could tweak. . . . [This reflection] made us become more efficient and effective with our processes. . . . If you had systems in place, you just had to tweak to make [them] electronic. . . . If you didn't have systems in place when you were brick and mortar, it really showed. I said to my district friends, Covid-19 has exposed the cubic zirconia. You are either going to be a diamond or you are going to be a cubic zirconia. Covid-19 has highlighted if you really have systems in place. If you didn't, it shows big time.

SYSTEM OF CURRICULUM AND INSTRUCTION

A system of curriculum and instruction is a large system that has a major impact on teachers and students. "Education and curriculum are connected and share a relationship in which both of them are enhanced" (Campbell-Phillips, 2020, p. 1075). Meaning, the curriculum serves as a roadmap for teachers and students, and when that curriculum is aligned to state standards and frequently updated, learning is improved.

So what constitutes a system of curriculum and instruction? According to Westberry (2020), components of this system, which must be progress monitored, include the following:

1. Curricular alignment to include the mapping of standards
2. Alignment of assessments to include formative, summative, and common assessments
3. Instructional alignment to include differentiated strategies
4. Use of data to inform instruction to include assessment data, observation data, lesson plan data, and professional learning community data
5. Focused remediation to include remediation and enrichment

These elements were discussed in chapter 7, but the elements need to be arranged and designed in order to inform instructional practices and student learning in a school.

Most schools have some semblance of a system of curriculum and instruction; however, often, elements are missing. For example, most districts provide a curriculum map for teachers. However, the constant revision of that curriculum and all of the elements of curriculum may be missing. Larry Ainsworth and Karen Donovan (2019) identify curricular elements to include the following: units of study, identification of priority and supporting standards, pacing calendar, unit plans, assessments, suggested instructional strategies, and resources.

Of course, some teachers prefer not to have such a defined curriculum because they feel they lose their creativity (Burnett & Smith, 2019). However, a defined curriculum does not dictate how a teacher chooses to teach the class. In fact creativity is limitless in this area. Administrators should encourage creativity because rote learning does not cognitively align to the standards, and learning should be fun. Not only do students prefer the creative classroom, but internal aspects of teacher self-efficacy and teacher creativity are positively correlated (Cayirdaq, 2017).

Once all elements of the system are defined, establishing how the system works in a building is critical. Just as one would map curriculum, an administrator should map the system utilizing all administrators and teacher leaders possible. The job of the principal is just too large for any one person to perform it effectively and efficiently. Once establishing the map of the system and how each element is progress monitored, an administrator should build the system to support the work. See Figure 8.1 for a sample system utilized by a South Carolina principal during the pandemic.

As stated earlier, each element must be progress monitored. Therefore, administrators have to work with teacher leaders to establish policy and practice in the school. For example, when are lesson plans submitted? Who reads them and what feedback is provided? Observation data? PLC data? A number of these issues were addressed in chapter 7, but that information needs to be further discussed to develop the system of how administrators respond when teachers are successful as well as when they are not. In turn, this same system helps teachers know how to respond to students when they are successful and when they are not.

For example, the simple task of observations needs to be planned and mapped. If not, administrators may default to quick walkthroughs in order to meet a minimum standard and check the box, rather than using observations as a tool for improvement. Imagine the administrator running to the gym to catch three physical education teachers in action and filling out three forms for the same time period. Three observations done in twenty minutes!

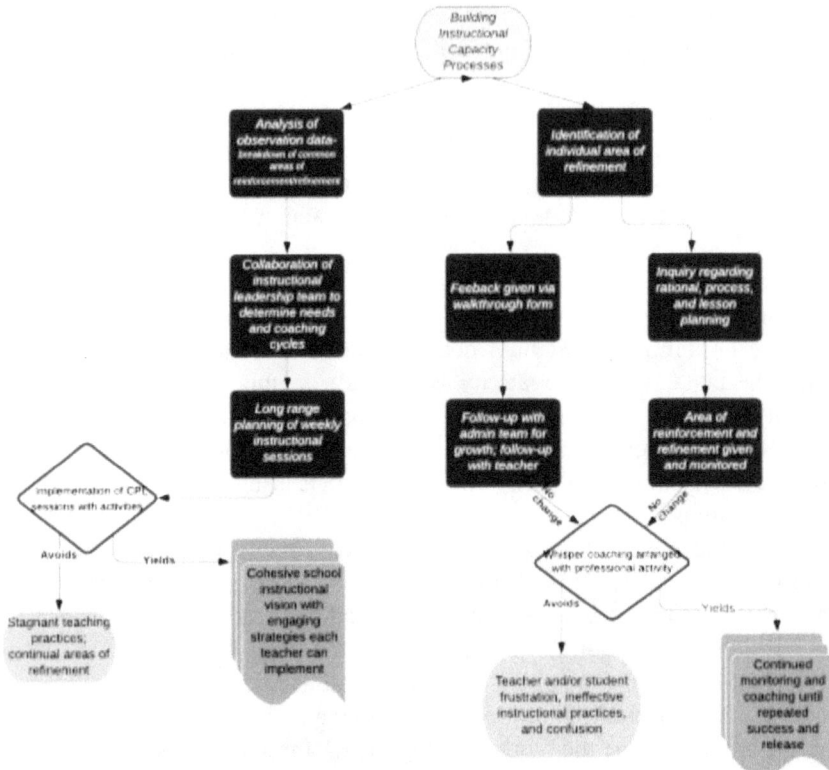

Figure 8.1 Sample curriculum and instruction system

Without a system, this really happens. See Figure 8.2 for a sample observation schedule that is planned.

Note that in the above table, the administrator directed the administrators to review lesson plans prior to observations. This practice provides the administrative team with valuable information, such as instruction and assessment alignment, student engagement, and so on. Additionally, the administrator instructed the team to provide feedback utilizing the evaluation rubric in South Carolina. This practice allows the team to come together and have real conversations about strengths and weaknesses in the building.

Also noted in the above example, each member of the team is assigned a group. In doing so, all teachers get observed rather than the same teachers time after time. These groups are staggered throughout the month so that all administrators see most groups each month. This is a great practice to work on interrater reliability as well, when at the end of the month members of the team can discuss observations of the same teachers. See a real example in the *Principal's Corner* below of how this system was managed during Covid.

WBECHS Walk-Through Schedule

	03/08	03/15	03/22	03/29	04/05	04/19
Dickson	7	8	1	2	3	4
McGrath	8	1	2	3	4	5
Cave	1	2	3	4	5	6
Kennedy	2	3	4	5	6	7
Garrett	3	4	5	6	7	8
Cato	4	5	6	7	8	1

Group 1-English	Group 2-Social Studies	Group 3-Science
Shannon Baker-Kahahelis	Corina Allen	Brian Powell
Feronica Hamilton-Pierce	William Edwards	Jessica Russell
Freda McCanick	Cameron King	Pretel Simmons-Hill
Hannah Stevenson	Brad Taracuk	Matthew Plantinga
Christine Williams	Willie White	
Group 4-Mathematics	**Group 5-FL/SPED**	**Group 6-CATE**
Derrick Barbee	Crystal Carpenter	Robert Carlin
Robert Bryant	Jane Emmett	Celine DiSalvo
Peter Burvenich	Kara Robinson	Joshua Ferguson
Portia Daise	Rebecca Schwenke	Pearl Mitchell
Rebecca Ginn		Sonia Perez-Robinson
Group 7-CATE/PE	**Group 8**	View Lesson Plans with academic feedback using the rubric.
Todd Stowe	Danielle Smalls	
John Williams	Skylah Sturgis	
Marvin Goodwin	Ashley Wright	
Jerry Hatcher	Frances Wright-Tellado	
Lee Jones		
James Raymond		

Figure 8.2 Sample observation schedule

Before Covid-19, the assistant principals, instructional coaches (academic and technology), and I would meet to discuss the data from surveys conducted in communities of professional learners (CPL), professional learning communities (PLCs), technology surveys, SCLEAD, and our walkthrough observation data. Then, we would triangulate the data and discuss the areas of reinforcement and refinement. Following this process, we would be able to have all voices of our faculty and staff to drive the decision on what our professional development strengths and challenges were as a whole and target those areas of refinement to build our capacity according to the 4.0 Teaching Rubrics.

When Covid-19 hit, the process did not change, but how we met did change. Instead of meeting face-to-face, we met on Zoom, shared the data, and discussed the indicators that we needed to strengthen to build our teachers' capacity, which directly affected our student achievement. This data drove our decisions on staff development, book/article studies (Covid-19 had us go to article studies), Warrior Institute, and possible response to teacher intervention (RTI). Yes, RTI for teachers leads to one-on-one coaching, whisper coaching with an instructional coach or administration inserted into a peer's classroom, or before or after school modeling. We did whatever it took to grow our teachers and build their capacity, which increases their self-efficacy and becomes an investment into the culture and climate of a school building. We follow the same process for our leadership meetings and administrative meetings.

Another aspect of Covid-19 made me review the setup of our leadership team and administrative team. Instead of having our teachers on the leadership team conduct walkthroughs and observations, our instructional coaches, assistant principals, athletic director, and principal completed the bulk of the observations in the school. Teachers only conducted formal observations for the school and ones requested by the administrative team within their content to assist the teacher.

Covid-19 assisted us in thinking outside the box, but the systems remained the same; they were just virtual and more efficient in analyzing data. Google forms for surveys assisted the process of analyzing the data. We became more strategic in what data we were studying, especially our processes, systems.

TEACHER SUPPORT SYSTEM

Teacher retention is a major issue that cannot be ignored. In fact, the teacher shortage is expected to continue and grow. One of the major reasons teachers leave the profession is lack of support (Zhang & Zeller, 2016). Teacher support systems should work to improve teaching and self-efficacy as well as provide humanistic support. Both of these areas need to be addressed in any system with teachers in order to retain them.

In a study by Reitman and Karge (2019), six support strategies emerged that have a direct impact on teacher retention:

1. Individual relationships
2. Pedagogical knowledge
3. Teacher self-efficacy
4. Mentoring
5. Professional learning
6. Reflection

Each of these areas should be considered when building a teacher support system. After all, teachers do not leave a school; they leave a school's leadership. Therefore, administrators should take special care to create this system, especially in the virtual realm when teachers feel more isolated.

These authors posit the list should be changed a bit. Teacher self-efficacy is extremely important, as it is the measure of how teachers feel their own confidence in being able to do their jobs. However, self-efficacy is built through the other strategies listed, plus one more. Therefore, the one additional element proposed to be added to the list is teacher leadership. In fact, these authors also recommend pedagogical knowledge and professional learning be combined into one along with reflecti.

Relationships

Relationships bring in the humanistic approach to leadership. Utilizing a humanistic psychological approach is based on the belief that people inherently want to perform well and have a positive impact; however, the whole person should be tended to, not just the sum of the parts (Buhler, 1971). In order to do so, administrators must look beyond the professional life of a teacher and see the whole person including motivations as well as barriers to achievement.

When administrators show they are truly invested in their staff, principals seek to understand their staff's personalities, home situations, health conditions, and so forth. For example, an administrator would not send an email because a teacher submitted lesson plans a day late if the principal knew the teacher was caring for a dying parent. That reminder email, even if friendly, could be the tipping point for the teacher. A better approach is to check in on the teacher and see how he/she could be supported through the trying time. Everyone has limits, and principals need to recognize the lives of teachers outside of school.

Understanding the lives of teachers also helps to build a personal relationship that creates a bond. Taking care of new teachers is especially important. This author has made doctor's appointments for new teachers and has been the emergency contact for many. When real relationships are formed out of support and respect, teachers do not want to leave that environment. Again, in the virtual realm, relationships are pivotal to teacher success because people feel more secure when relationships exist.

Pedagogical Knowledge, Professional Learning, and R

Helping to build a teacher's pedagogical knowledge is very important. Teachers are students, by their very nature. Therefore, teachers want to be shown "how" to do something, like differentiate and use engaging technologies. They do not want to be told to do it, and then they are left to figure it out on their own. Providing quality ongoing professional development (PD) is a staple support for teachers. The pandemic only highlighted this need.

Administrators who take the lead on providing that PD and those who utilize the resources within their building to provide additional development have the greatest impact. Let's apply this to the pandemic. When the world went virtual, teachers were made to not only provide curriculum virtually, but also teach virtually. If teachers did not have the pedagogical knowledge on how to engagingly teach in the virtual environment and principals were not providing the needed support, teachers and students were frustrated. Therefore, achievement was impacted, and many students have likely fallen behind (Kwakye & Kibort-Crocker, 2021).

When considering PD, one must consider the cycles of PD needed. Chapter 7 discussed all of the cycles of PD, but these cycles must be mapped into a system. See Table 8.1 below for a sample simple map of the multiple cycles of PD. Remember, new teachers deserve the training others received in years prior if the instructional expectation remains. Also focused PD can be for those who need additional help, for specific departments, or for those accelerated teachers. Either way, focused PD can be invitation only.

In the below simple map, new teachers were provided PD on differentiating instruction and literacy strategies in the classroom. Since others were not receiving this PD on these instructional priorities, training had previously been provided. However, new teachers will certainly benefit from the learning. All-teacher PD was clearly focused on integrating technology in instruction. Focused PD included differentiation, for those suggested to attend, because those invited may struggle with differentiation. Lastly, science teachers were the only teachers invited to the science notebook training.

Determining PD needs based on data, as previously discussed, as well as utilizing teacher input is important. However, one must not forget the cycles

Table 8.1 Sample Map of Cycles of PD

PD	All Teachers	New Teachers	Focused PD
Setting up Google Classroom	8/18/2020 Zoom Link		
Literacy Strategies in the Classroom		9/1/2020 Zoom Link	
Google Classroom Assignments and Assessments	9/14/2020 Zoom Link		
Differentiating Instruction		9/27/2020 Zoom Link	9/27/2020 Zoom Link
Flipgrid, Kami, and Mural in the Classroom	10/1/2020 Zoom Link		
Science Notebooks			10/8/2020 Zoom Link
Jamboard, Padlet, and Kahoot in the Classroom	10/17/2020 Zoom Link		

of PD. All cycles need to run concurrently in a school year, so mapping the PD and the dates/times is pivotal to a program's success. Teachers should have the map at the beginning of the year, so they know where and when to attend the sessions needed to continue their professional growth. By being given advance notice, teachers can plan ahead and mark their calendars.

In the virtual world, this professional learning should not stop. The same PD can be provided virtually for teachers, and the use of video and technologies like Zoom and Google Meets make it that much easier. The catch is that those providing the PD should be able to model the engaging technologies expected in the classroom. So administrative learning is also required.

Hudson, a high school principal with three years of experience, describes his school's approach to systematizing professional development in the following excerpt:

> Modeling the model. When our instructional team does professional development, they try to model some of the best practices in engaging teachers just like we would hope teachers are engaging their students. . . . It takes a lot of time, but we've tried to do what we call personalized professional development because we know that our teachers are in such different places, again modeling the model, because our students are also in such different places. We meet the teacher where they are. A teacher who was one of the most dynamic teachers face-to-face may be one of the least dynamic teachers because they don't have the skills. And I always go back to a skill gap versus a will gap. I think in most cases you see teachers who have a skill gap . . . and so with our personalized PD we're really meeting them where they are.

Don't also forget that professional learning communities (PLCs) provide valuable development from peers. PLCs, defined, are collaborative groups of teachers who meet to learn from one another through sharing and critical *reflective* practice that promote learning (Mitchell & Sackney, 2000; Toole & Louis, 2002). When considering Covid, the practice of PLCs should not diminish. In fact, sharing one another's challenges to develop solutions and connecting to others are important parts of teacher learning in times of isolation.

Therefore, PLCs should be scheduled for teachers with expected outcomes or protocol so that administrators can use that information to further inform professional learning needs. In the virtual world, administrators are more likely to have time to attend PLCs than they would in a normal setting. This PLC continued practice supports connections not only to other teachers but also with administration, which is pivotal in times of change.

Teacher Leadership

Another way to show support with professional learning is to tap teachers in the building or virtual environment who exceed expectations in a skill set. For example, in the above map, a principal could ask a couple of teachers who are great with differentiation of instruction to provide the PD to the new teachers. Not only do the new teachers gain support, but the tenured teachers feel valued by the administration. Utilizing teacher leadership is an essential part of teacher support.

Teacher leadership has been positively correlated with educator commitment and job satisfaction, academic capacity, and teacher effectiveness (Bellibas & Liu, 2018; Liu & Werblow, 2019). In the context of committee meetings, such as school improvement councils and leadership teams, teacher leaders should be running these meetings. Administrators should be a part of the committees, certainly, but teachers should have real input in how the school operates.

Multiple committees or groups may exist within a building, and this is optimal. The work should be shared among the staff. According to Price's Law, the square root of the number of people in the organization perform half of the work, as the law is applied to work (Rathika, Thanuskodi, & Sudhakar, 2020). So, in a school of one hundred teachers, according to Price's Law, ten staff members perform half of the work of the school, while the other ninety perform the other half of the work. Imagine that in that ninety, many are completely inactive. Therefore, it is important to develop capacity in the building among the staff.

Mentoring

Mentoring is another mode of professional learning and support for teachers, especially new and struggling teachers. Most mentor programs in schools are for new teachers; however, these authors postulate that all new teachers to a building, whether they have prior experience or not, as well as struggling teachers should have a mentor assigned to them. Obviously, new teachers to the profession need mentors. In a 2017 study by Sparks and colleagues, new-teacher mentoring was shown to improve pedagogical and professional outcomes.

Furthermore, one cannot assume that teachers with prior experience have the experience you need in your building. For example, instructional expectations are not equal among districts and even within districts. Therefore, a principal should never assume that an experienced teacher will not have struggles or challenges adjusting. Mentors can lessen the degree of struggle and build relationships among the new staff.

Lastly, struggling teachers deserve mentors, too. Too often, teachers who struggle meeting expectations are put on an improvement plan that requires them to attend professional development sessions and meet certain benchmarks. However, rarely are these teachers assigned a mentor to help them navigate the change needed prior to being placed on an improvement plan. In fact, Erichsen and Reynolds (2020) found that accountability measures, such as improvement plans for teachers, often undermine the goal of improving teacher performance. Therefore, teacher mentors are pivotal for teachers who struggle, and Covid presented many struggles.

STUDENT SUPPORT SYSTEM

Student support systems are necessary in order to "catch" kids before they fall through the cracks. These cracks can be social and emotional cracks, academic cracks, and cracks due to home and community environments. Therefore, administrators need to fully develop these systems because today's children face more challenges than many can imagine. Covid-19 highlighted many of these challenges, and more students have fallen behind, particularly those from marginalized communities (Lee & Morling, 2020).

As stated in chapter 5, students from split homes, low-income homes, or foster homes may live without a constant support in their lives (Baker, 2020). Therefore, schools are often the single source of support for children, and Covid-19 made that support more difficult to provide. Student support systems should be inclusive of guidance, multi-tiered systems of support (MTSS), mentoring, and outside agencies.

Guidance

According to the American School Counselor Association (2012), guidance counselors should spend 80 percent of their time in direct and indirect services to students. In a normal school setting, counselors are often inundated with administrivia and often do not get to allocate the time needed for counseling services. Some of those services, particularly in the virtual environment, might include the following: small groups and graduation plans. Support for at-risk groups can be part of the small group program.

Small Groups

Small group counseling is designed to support students around a particular issue. Students in the group share the same issue (truancy, teenage pregnancy, academic failures, poor choices, etc.) in a safe and inclusive environment

(Gerrity & DeLucia-Waack, 2006), and counselors work with students in order to teach them coping mechanisms, differing strategies, and alternative choices. Students, outside of these groups, often feel alone, and the group provides them a sense of belonging (Tucker et al., 2019).

During Covid-19, many students experienced elevated levels of anxiety and depression that were associated with the isolation and the stress of virtual schooling (Gosku et al., 2021; McGuine et al., 2021). Small groups could easily be conducted virtually, but first a social/emotional screener for all students may be necessary. If teachers are not in tune with their students, the screener may reveal students in need that mere grades and attendance did not reveal. Guidance could divvy up the students in need and conduct checks and small group counseling.

Of course, counselors would need to inform administration and teachers of the students in need so that they could keep watch for those students as well. The combined effort of school staff coupled with small group counseling can have a lasting impact on students academically, behaviorally, and emotionally.

Graduation Planning

Despite Covid, student graduation plans for high school students still needed to be conducted. Counselors conduct these conferences with students and parents, preferably. Of course, some video conferencing technology was needed in order to complete this task. Since graduation plans are not a onetime event but occur every year in high school until a student graduates, the use of technology may continue in the future due to ease. However, Covid-19's impact on students extended to this realm as well.

As discussed earlier, most students have fallen behind and have suffered learning losses, but students of color are faring worse (Dorn et al., 2020; Engzell, Frey, & Verhagen, 2021). Counseling students on grades and academic achievement along with career and college options is inevitable in a graduation plan meeting. During these meetings, course selection for the following year is also discussed to ensure courses are in line with college choices and majors. For some students, this counseling may have spurred them to work harder.

MTSS

MTSS is a support structure that systemically moves students to different levels of prevention and support depending on their academic and behavioral needs. These interventions are tiered and increase in intensity (Center on Response to Intervention at American Institutes for Research, 2014). This continuum of support was highly needed during Covid and will probably be needed even more when students return to school.

In order to effectively use MTSS in a virtual setting, educators must fully understand the three tiers of support that are used to guide student continuous improvement. The efforts should be collaborative among teachers and ongoing. See Figure 8.3 to understand the three tiers of an academic program support.

Tier 1 interventions are meant for all students in the school. This level constitutes the educational foundation, or core curriculum, and behavioral supports for all students. What is often overlooked is that Tier 1 also includes accommodations that all students can receive. Tier 1 should be the richest tier, based on the resources available in the school. For example, tutoring is a Tier 1 intervention because all children have access to it.

Tier 2 interventions comprise small group instruction/counseling, specially designed courses, varied instructional materials, and so on. Students who are unsuccessful in Tier 1 after multiple interventions are utilized may move to Tier 2. However, progress needs to be monitored and data needs to be shared among the collaboration of teachers serving students in Tier 2.

The final tier, Tier 3, requires more intensive, personalized interventions. This may include one-on-one assistance in the classroom or with counseling services. For example, a reading specialist may work with a Tier 3 student. Again, all interventions must be progress monitored and reported.

So, during Covid, how did school MTSS systems fare? Social/emotional interventions may have been utilized as heavily as academic interventions. However, they were not all successful. Because of the learning losses previously discussed that are facing the nation, Tier 1 interventions may not have been sufficient. A fully developed Tier 1 incorporates many accommodations

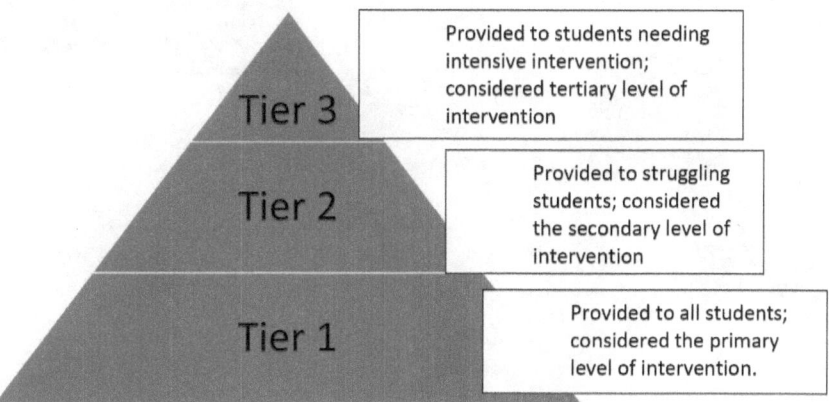

Figure 8.3 MTSS three tiers of support (Westberry, 2020, p. 23)

to help the struggling learner. Too often, schools do not have a rich Tier 1, and this results in more kids being recommended for testing.

Principals must work with teachers to design a program that is rich, and teachers must understand a process for recommendation for MTSS as well as the data requirements. The process should include multiple accommodations and interventions tried before the first referral is made. The seamless system is intended to prevent deep struggles, as signs of struggle are recognized immediately. See Figure 8.4 below for a sample social/emotional system utilized in one school during Covid.

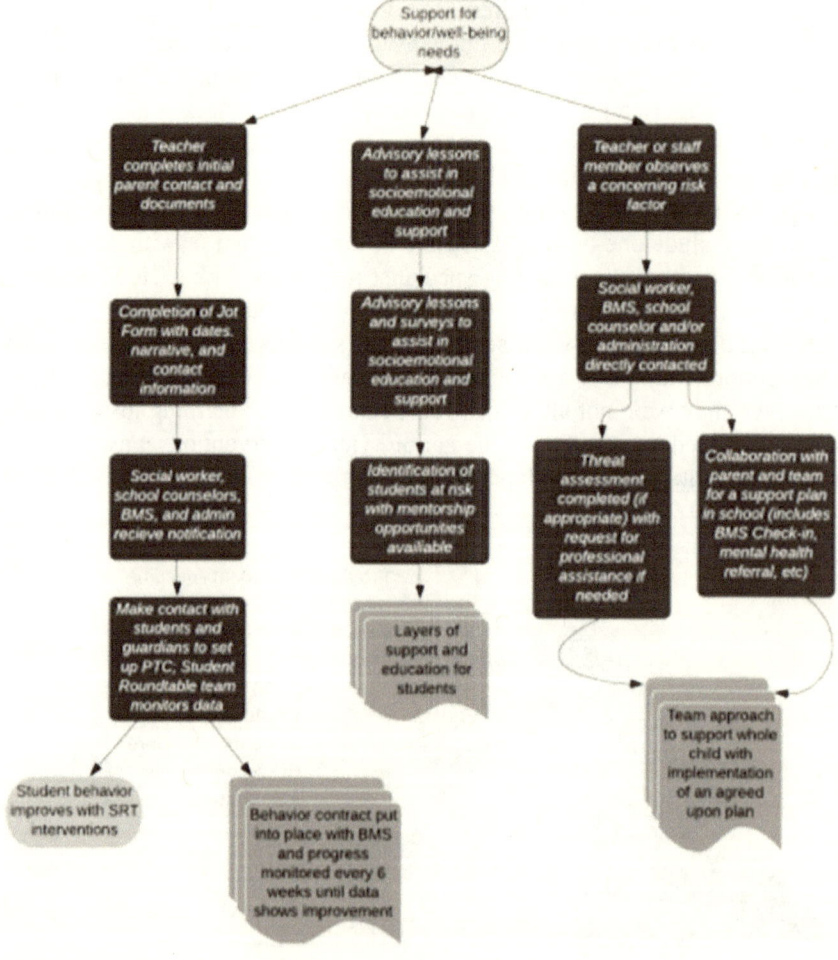

Figure 8.4 Sample MTSS system for social/emotional indicators

Mentoring

Mentoring programs are not new but mentoring virtually may be just that. Schools utilize mentoring programs at all grade levels, from elementary to high school. Some schools utilize teachers and staff to mentor students with a defined curriculum, while other schools utilize outside agencies, such as the local Rotary Club, to provide mentors for children. In either case, mentors need to know the expectations for their time spent with children, and they need to be trained properly.

Virtually, these same mentoring programs should be utilized. A school schedule can be adjusted for mentor days to allow time separate from regular class time for mentoring. The best practice is for students to keep the same mentor throughout their tenure at a particular school. This means, students in middle school should have the same mentor for all middle grades. The same is true for high school. A long-term mentor relationship yields better results for the student in terms of attendance, attitude toward school, and opportunities post high school (Tierney, Grossman, & Resch, 1995).

Outside Agencies

Dryfoos (2005) stated that schools alone cannot address all of the problems and needs of disadvantaged children. However, schools are responsible to ensure achievement for all students, despite the inequities in resources and family support some children suffer. Schools cannot do it alone. Therefore, it is important to take stock of the outside agencies in your area that can assist in meeting the needs of students and families.

Counselors should have at their fingertips a list of state and local agencies that can support students and families. Educational programs for students and parents should also be developed based on the needs presented. For example, a parent meeting with a child psychologist on how to help their ADHD child could be beneficial. An agency on speed dial that can help to find housing for a student who suddenly becomes homeless is definitely needed.

These agencies, in a brick and mortar or virtual setting, need to be utilized for the benefit of children. If students' basic needs are not being met, those students cannot be expected to learn as well as others. Think about Maslow's Hierarchy of Needs (Maslow, 1970). If the basic needs of safety and shelter are not met, a student cannot focus on science.

CULTURE SYSTEM

Culture is created, and it should be intentional. If you plan to fail for culture, you plan to fail. This culture system includes a growth mindset among teachers and students, community support, and district support. Creating a system of communication, professional learning, high expectations with a strong system of MTSS, and so on, all play into building a culture. Communication is a key factor in this system as well.

In Figure 8.5 below, a principal designed a system to develop relationships with students and parents while showing the desire to truly support kids. Relationships began as soon as students entered the school at the lowest grade level (i.e., ninth grade for high school). The principal in this situation planned for continuous communication coming from the school as well as taking that communication to the community in church forums and township meetings.

The point is to plan the communication and interactions so that the community can understand the school's efforts. If people understand the "why" behind an initiative, they typically can support it. In the absence of communication, people are left to their own interpretations. These interpretations, left

Figure 8.5 Sample system of building culture through relationships

misguided, may be counterproductive to the school's vision and may serve as an obstacle to progress.

The same is true for teachers. If teachers understand the "why" behind an initiative and how that initiative will benefit students, most teachers will support it. In developing a growth mindset with teachers, communication is also a large part of the process. The communication should always resonate the same message: Whatever it takes to support kids. For students, the same message needs to resonate in the school and the community: Yes, you can and you will!

If the administrator has a growth mindset in always looking to improve, and the systems are in place to support improvement (refer to three prior systems), then teachers develop a growth mindset. The trickle down effect is that when teachers possess a desire to grow, that desire is transferred to students. This is true because teachers do not allow students to fail quietly when best practices in teaching and assessment are sought. Therefore, communication has to be deliberate, planned, and focused to support a growth mindset in the school and community. This is true in a normal setting, but communication is even more critical in a virtual setting.

SUMMARY

A systems approach dictates that the whole of the organization is considered as well as how each part impacts the whole. In addition to ripple effects, systemic approaches in schools invite collaboration and shared decision making.

There are four major systems in schools: curriculum and instruction, teacher support, student support, and culture. Each system has a profound impact on the others, and no one can be ignored to maximize effectiveness. Virtual principals as well as traditional principals must plan each component of all four systems.

Curriculum and instruction systems include curricular alignment of standards, curricular units, all assessments, instructional strategies, data-informed decision making, and focused remediation. A systems approach to curriculum and instruction would be incomplete without progress-monitoring tools that can be utilized virtually.

Teacher support systems not only help with teacher retention, but also improve teaching and learning. This system includes elements such as the following: pedagogical knowledge and professional learning, teacher leadership, and mentoring. Again, elements for each of these components must be planned and progress monitored virtually.

Student support systems include guidance systems, MTSS, mentoring, and outside agency support. Each element, again, must be planned. Remember, teacher leadership should be utilized to help build these systems and operate them. Procedures and processes must be defined clearly.

A culture system should be planned to include multiple avenues of communication with teachers, students, and the community in order to build a growth mindset. The three prior systems, if designed well, also contribute to that growth mindset. In the virtual, communication is most critical.

POLISHING THE DIAMOND

1. What are the four major systems in schools?
2. Describe four elements of a system of curriculum and instruction and describe how you would progress monitor them.
3. Name and describe three ways teachers gain pedagogical knowledge.
4. How do you progress monitor teacher learning?
5. What teachers should receive a teacher mentor and why?
6. Name and describe two ways guidance can support students.
7. Describe an MTSS system? What is it and how does it work?
8. How can a mentoring system be implemented virtually?
9. What is the most important component of a culture system and why?

REFERENCES

Ainsworth, L., & Donovan, K. (2019). *Rigorous curriculum design: How to create curricular units of study that align to standards, instruction, and assessment.* Rexford, NY: International Center for Leadership in Education.

American School Counselor Association (2012). *ASCA National Model: A framework for school counseling programs* (3rd edition). Alexandria, VA: Author.

Amsler, L., & O'Leary, R. (2017). Collaborative public management and systems thinking. *International Journal of Public Sector Management, 30*(6–7), 626–639.

Baker, J. (2020, April 12). The kids who will never return to school after COVID-19. *Sydney Morning Herald.* Available from https://www.smh.com.au/national/the-kids-who-will-never-return-toschool-after-covid-19-20200411-p54j0e.html

Bellibas, M. S., & Liu, Y. (2018). The effects of principals' perceived instructional and distributed leadership practices on their perceptions of school climate. *International Journal of Leadership in Education, 21*(2), 226–244.

Buhler, C. (1971). Basic theoretical concepts of humanistic psychology. *American Psychologist, 26*(4), 378–386.

Burnett C., & Smith S. (2019) Reaching for the star: A model for integrating creativity in education. In C. Mullen (ed.), *Creativity under duress in education? Creativity theory and action in education*, Vol 3. Cham, Switzerland: Springer.

Cabrera, D., & Cabrera, L. (2019). Complexity and systems thinking models in education: Applications for leaders. *Learning, Design, and Technology: An International Compendium of Theory, Research, Practice, and Policy*, 1–29.

Campbell-Phillips, S. (2020). Education and curriculum reform: The impact they have on learning. *Budapest International Research and Critics in Linguistics and Education Journal, 3*(2), 1074–1082.

Cayirdag, N. (2017). Creativity fostering teaching: Impact of creative self-efficacy and teacher efficacy. *Educational Sciences: Theory & Practice, 17*(6).

Center on Response to Intervention at American Institutes for Research. (2014). *Response to intervention glossary of terms.* Washington, DC: Author. Retrieved from http://www.rti4success.org/sites/default/files/CenterOnRTIGlossary.pdf

Dorn, E., Hancock, B., Sarakatsannis, J., & Viruleg, E. (2020). *COVID-19 and learning loss—Disparities grow and students need help.* McKinsey & Company, *December 8.* Accessed https://www.mckinsey.com/industries/public-and-social-sector/our-insights/covid-19-and-learning-loss-disparities-grow-and-students-need-help

Dryfoos, J. (2005). Full-service community schools: A strategy—not a program. *New Directions for Youth Cevelopment,* (107), 7–14.

Engzell, P., Frey, A., & Verhagen, M. D. (2021). From the Cover: Learning loss due to school closures during the COVID-19 pandemic. *Proceedings of the National Academy of Sciences of the United States of America, 118*(17).

Erichsen, K., & Reynolds, J. (2020). Public school accountability, workplace culture, and teacher morale. *Social Science Research, 85*, 102347.

Gerrity, D. A., & DeLucia-Waack, J. L. (2006). Effectiveness of groups in the schools. *The Journal for Specialists in Group Work, 32*, 97–106.

Göksu, İ., Ergün, N., Özkan, Z., & Sakız, H. (2021). Distance education amid a pandemic: Which psycho-demographic variables affect students in higher education? *Journal of Computer Assisted Learning.* https://doi.org/10.1111/jcal.12544

Jaaron, A., & Backhouse, C. (2014). Service organizations resilience through the application of the vanguard method of systems thinking: A case study approach. *International Journal of Production Research, 52*(7), 2026–2041.

Kwakye, I., & Kibort-Crocker, E. (2021). *Facing learning disruption: Examining the effects of the COVID-19 pandemic on K–12 students.* Washington, DC: Washington Student Achievement Council.

Lee, A., & Morling, J. (2020). Coronavirus disease 2019: Emerging lessons from the pandemic. *Public Health.* doi:10.1016/j.puhe.2020.05.012.

Liu, Y., Werblow, J. (2019). The operation of distributed leadership and the relationship with organizational commitment and job satisfaction of principals and teachers: A multi-level model and meta-analysis using the 2013 TALIS data. *International Journal of Educational Research, 96*, 41–55.

Maslow, A. H. (1970). *Motivation and personality* (2nd ed.). New York: Harper and Row.

McGuine, T. A., Biese, K. M., Petrovska, L., Hetzel, S. J., Reardon, C., Kliethermes, S., & Watson, A. M. (2021). Mental health, physical activity, and quality of life of US adolescent athletes during COVID-19–related school closures and sport cancellations: A study of 13000 athletes. *Journal of Athletic Training, 56*(1), 11–19.

Mitchell, C., & Sackney, L. (2000). *Profound improvement: Building capacity for a learning community*. Lisse, Netherlands: Swets and Zeitlinger.

Randle, J. M., & Stroink, M. L. (2018). The development and initial validation of the paradigm of systems thinking. *Systems Research and Behavioral Science, 35*(6), 645–657.

Rathika, N., Thanuskodi, S., & Sudhakar, K. (2020). Lotka's law and the patter of scientific productivity in the marine pollution research. *International Journal of Emerging Technologies, 11*(2), 332–334.

Reitman, G. C., & Karge, B. D. (2019). Investing in teacher support leads to teacher retention: Six supports administrators should consider for new teachers. *Multicultural Education, 27*(1), 7–18.

Shaked, H., & Schechter, C. (2020). Systems thinking leadership: New explorations for school improvement. *Management in Education, 34*(3), 107–114.

Sparks, J., Tsemenhu, R., Green, R., Truby, W., Brockmeier, L. L., & Noble, K. D. (2017). Investigating new teacher mentoring practices. *National Teacher Education Journal, 10*(1), 59–65.

Tierney, J., Grossman, J., & Resch, N. A. N. C. Y. (1995). *Making a difference: An impact study of Big Brothers, Big Sisters.*

Toole, J., & Louis, K. (2002). The role of the professional learning communities in international education. In K. Leithwood and P. Hallinger (eds.), *Second international handbook of educational leadership and administration*. Dordrecht, Netherlands: Kluwer.

Tucker, J. R., Wade, N. G., Abraham, W. T., Bitman-Heinrichs, R. L., Cornish, M. A., & Post, B. C. (2019). Modeling cohesion change in group counseling: The role of client characteristics, group variables, and leader behaviors. *Journal of Counseling Psychology*. Advance online publication. https://doi.org/10.1037/cou0000403

Westberry, L. (2020). *Putting the pieces together: A systems approach to school leadership*. Lanham, MD: Rowman & Littlefield.

Zhang, G., & Zeller, N. (2016). A longitudinal investigation of the relationship between teacher preparation and teacher retention. *Teacher Education Quarterly, 43*(2), 73–92.

Chapter 9

Challenges and Successes

If it doesn't challenge you, it doesn't change you.

—Fred Devito

CHALLENGES

Principals navigated numerous challenges during the rapid transition to virtual principalship during the Covid-19 pandemic. Some of the most significant challenges reported by principals were in the areas of social and emotional support for teachers and staff and students and their families, as well as self-care. Principals also reported navigating robust challenges in fostering student engagement, ensuring student achievement, and ensuring effective implementation and utilization of technologies during the shift to virtual instruction.

SOCIAL/EMOTIONAL SUPPORT AND SELF-CARE

During the transition to virtual principalship, leaders found themselves in brand-new territory. As if transitioning an entire organization to virtual operations was not challenging enough, principals also found themselves entrenched in helping to navigate through fears related to the Covid-19 pandemic as well as ensuring their school's health and safety.

Central to leading during the crisis, principals had expanded responsibilities related to the social-emotional needs of teachers, students, and parents, as well as their own families (Anderson, Hayes, & Carpenter, 2020; Kaul, VanGronigen, & Simon, 2020). As a principal, you often have to think of the school community before yourself as part of the family unit, and during the pandemic, this was made even more difficult.

For example, imagine a school is identified as a hurricane shelter for a community, as so many are. If a hurricane was predicted to make landfall in that community, the principal would have to stay with the school and community members. His or her family, however, may evacuate without the leader. These types of distinctions are made all too often, and they can be difficult to navigate.

Principals quickly found they had to address the basic physiological and safety needs of students and teachers before progress could be made in the shift to virtual instruction and ensuring student learning. Of course, principals were also dealing with the emotional toll and health and safety of their own families simultaneously.

Kay, an experienced high school principal, notes the importance of providing encouragement to teachers and constantly communicating, "You can do this." Jack, a first-year principal, highlights the types of messages he used that were central to addressing physiological and safety needs within the learning community:

> Take care of yourself, your mental health. I check with my teachers all the time. I'm doing surveys or I'm walking by, [and] I'm asking them what's going on? Is there anything that I can help you with?

Witnessing the widespread fear of many teachers, students, and parents in navigating the Covid-19 virus as well as its health and economic impacts on their communities also took a toll on principals' social and emotional well-being and level of stress (Anderson, Hayes, & Carpenter, 2020). Hanna, an experienced high school principal, shares,

> It's mentally fatiguing, I think because you're just, it's more mental. It's not physical. It's mental. It's the emotional of it too. I mean, I feel like I'm emotionally depleted because you give so much all day and you worry, you worry. I mean, I worry all the time about my teachers and I worry about my kids and I worry about all of that and are we doing what we need to do for everybody?

Kay, an experienced high school principal, notes that this type of fatigue can make principals feel "angry and alone. You feel alone sometimes in this position. You can't share, so you're alone." Kay elaborates on what principals can do to foster greater self-care in these situations:

> Have grace for yourself, as much as you do for others. Know that you're going to make mistakes, but as long as you learn from those mistakes and you admit to those mistakes and say, "Hey, before I'm just gonna try something else," I think

it goes a long way. And I really feel like . . . I am big on giving grace to others and I think I have a pretty good culture here at my school in terms of them trusting me. And sometimes you have to, as the leader, be able to trust those around you a little more too, that they're going to take care of you.

STUDENT ENGAGEMENT AND ACHIEVEMENT

Principals consistently reported student engagement and achievement as major challenges during the transition to virtual instruction. The abrupt shift to virtual instruction necessitated the quick development of policies and strategies for improving the student learning experience and ensuring accountability. These policies and strategies proved critical as schools experienced challenges with Zoom behavior, absenteeism, and increasing numbers of students needing to work due to pandemic-related family job losses.

Learning loss is also a significant concern among principals. Numerous research studies have utilized absentee, online learning, and summer learning loss data to project significant learning loss due to the Covid-19 pandemic (Dorn et al., 2020; Kuhfeld & Tarasawa, 2020; Kuhfeld et al., 2020). Using absenteeism and summer learning data from over five million students, projections indicate a 63 percent to 68 percent learning gain in reading and 37 percent to 50 percent learning gain in math relative to prepandemic years (Kuhfeld et al., 2020).

Principals are also worried about a widening achievement gap due to the transition to virtual learning. Given the differences in technology resources and utilization of virtual instruction, some schools were better prepared for the transition to virtual learning than others. An increasing number of research studies are indicating unequal levels of learning loss and a widening achievement gap (Dorn et al., 2020; Kuhfeld et al., 2020; Kuhfeld & Tarasawa, 2020).

Student engagement is a critical element in knowledge acquisition and student retention. Principals had to quickly reimagine what strong student engagement would look like for their school in the virtual environment. Central to this was creating a cohesive and strong sense of community. Christina, a school superintendent with extensive experience, shares,

> The barrier of not having the physical contact with a student is really tough. You know, as much as we have upgraded our microphones, upgraded our cameras, I've seen students really retreat there with different kids. They haven't had a chance to find their social niche. And I really feel that that's the biggest

challenge for us right now is that social and emotional engagement, particularly with our virtual students.

Similarly, Donna, a high school principal with three years of experience, shares about strategies and challenges in engaging students from behind a computer screen or phone:

> We did start doing a Monday meeting with all of our virtual students and we made them log in and we had about an hour meeting every Monday to start teaching skills and talking to them about those skills. But what I found is even in those meetings, I had students renovating houses and students in the car driving somewhere. It was hard to prepare them for that because we didn't see them every day as a virtual principal. I would think that would be the hardest part. . . . How do you teach those skills that students need when they're sitting behind a computer at home?

In the quantitative component of the mixed-method study, principals and superintendents reported significant professional development needs in understanding how to effectively progress monitor as a virtual principal, with over 84 percent of all principals and superintendents reporting moderate to very high support needs in this area. Over 75 percent of all principals in the study also reported the need for additional professional development in understanding how to implement successful multi-tiered systems of support programs in the virtual world.

TECHNOLOGY

Principals faced a multitude of technology-related challenges during the transition to virtual instruction. These challenges included the procurement and deployment of technology, evaluation and adoption of technology best practices, implementation, and technology training for teachers and students. Principals had to make critical decisions. Will our school offer virtual-only instruction? Will our school provide virtual and in-person instruction? Should our school offer a hybrid option?

The answers each principal found to these questions often drove their own sets of challenges. For example, Christina, a school superintendent with extensive experience, shares,

> We are operating in dual modality, which means every single one of our classes is offered both virtually and in person at the same time. So that is the single biggest challenge. Now for teachers it is making sure that they have the instructional acumen of how to engage both sets of students.

The majority of principals in the study described significant efforts in assessing students' and teachers' access to technology. In many cases, principals had to provide Wi-Fi hot spots or Wi-Fi subscriptions for students and teachers to address the digital divide of internet access in this country. Access to laptops and notepads also had to be evaluated and addressed.

Technology training for teachers and students was also a major challenge. Principals quickly found a wide continuum of technology skills within their workforce. The lack of online teaching or training in online instruction also was a complicating factor. For example, Jack, a first-year principal, highlights, "The technology was in place, but most of our teachers have not taken any educational courses in college that taught them to teach virtually." Likewise, Donna, a high school principal with three years of experience, shares,

> Buildings, internet access, Chromebooks programs, but it didn't matter because you didn't get the training and you didn't have the time to learn those programs and how to use any of that technology. And so [districts] were quick to provide us with [technology], but a lot of teachers didn't know what to do with it or how to use it.

In the mixed-method study, leaders noted the importance of virtual principals developing strong knowledge of technology capabilities as a critical knowledge foundation. Most interview respondents also expressed the need for additional professional development in better understanding current and emerging technologies to better serve their students and teachers. This growth mindset approach will aid virtual principals' ability to plan for their schools' future technologies.

SUCCESSES

Social/Emotional Support

Though there were many challenges faced by administrators during the Covid-19 pandemic, there were also many successes that arose from the shift to virtual leadership. The first among them is the social and emotional support of staff. In contradiction to the quarantine status, emotional support increased when faculty and administration were physically separated.

Teams were strengthened throughout the process, and the lessons learned should continue when all are fully back in the brick-and-mortar school setting. The pandemic caused administrators to stop and think and act more supportively more often. Jack, a first-year principal, stated,

You have to learn to take care of yourself while taking care of others. You not only need to check in frequently with your staff, but you need to do a personal check in as well. Continually offering assistance is important, but it is also important to ask for assistance when needed. Teachers appreciate it when you do.

These simple acts mean a great deal to teachers.

Teaching is already an emotionally demanding profession (Somech, 2016), and teachers can feel intense stress from the ever-increasing demands placed upon them from students, parents, administration, legislation, and so on (Day, 2013). Research already shows that emotional/social support can alleviate the negative effects of the workplace (Almeida et al., 2016), and logic dictates those normal stressors may have been magnified during the Covid shutdown and switch to virtual learning. So better communication was imperative.

Even though many principals act as a buffer for teachers, the best way to reduce stress is through proper, supportive communication strategies (Berkovich & Eyal, 2018), and principals should consider these strategies in a normal setting. In fact, a positive emotional culture that is communicated enhances an organization's identity (Yue, Men, & Ferguson, 2021). That organizational identity can then become one of a supportive team, which is certainly conducive to maximum effectiveness.

So remembering to take the time to develop strong communication strategies is crucial for teacher support, pandemic or not. Consider surveys, fireside chats, one-on-one conversations, small group discussions, personal notes, emails, and the like. Build the system that shows teachers you care and are there for them. The effort is minimal compared to the reward.

TECHNOLOGY PROFICIENCY

As stated earlier, the virtual Pandora's Box has been opened. Though schools may not be in the same predicament again as with Covid-19, hopefully, virtual elements are here to stay. Teachers who were once technologically deficient have had to become technologically proficient, and this is true of administrators as they have had to become technology leaders. This change has been positive since technology integration is seen as vital to preparation for the twenty-first-century workforce (Jan, 2017).

Donna, a high school principal with three years of experience, states,

> We've learned a lot about virtual and a lot of the opportunities that are out there that we may be able to offer to our students now. All of my teachers are now proficient with technology. We have primarily veteran teachers here that if you would have told them a year ago, they were going to do virtual classes, they

would have retired. But it's the learning curve. It's taken a while, but most of them are proficient and can easily shut down a classroom and run it from home within thirty minutes to forty-five minutes. And so that's definitely been a success for us.

So, with this technology proficiency, which is defined as the ability to use technology to communicate, organize information, and further enhance thinking skills, teachers will have more time to be creative and support innovation (Saad & Sankaran, 2020).

What could this look like in schools and in the classroom? Administrators could video meetings to share with faculty, who then can view them in their own time. This practice could save actual face-to-face meeting time for professional development, thereby reducing the number of missed planning periods. Teachers can more easily flip classrooms, which is more focused on active learning and student engagement. In flipped classrooms, teachers may provide the direct instruction through video, and then classroom time can be spent on the student engagement with the knowledge wherein the teacher acts as a facilitator (Rasheed et al., 2020).

The sheer act of using applications such as Zoom or Google Meets implies many increased applications in schools and districts such as video conferencing for PLCs that can connect teachers from different schools, video conferencing for parent meetings, video conferencing for district meetings that prevent removing administrators from the buildings, and so on. Because of its ease of use and now more widespread application, the use of video conferencing may become a staple. Think of the application for tutoring accessibility!

Virtual learning platforms, which have been used as a platform for students at home during the pandemic, may also continue to be used in a hybrid or blended learning approach. Since teacher acceptance to use an online platform is based on their technology readiness, the biggest hurdle has been cleared at this point.

As mentioned in chapter 5, administrators will need to stay abreast of technological trends and new programs available. Students will continue to expect technology's use in the classroom, and teachers need to be ready for whatever comes next. This requires principals to provide quality professional development on technology that is ongoing.

CULTURE OF CHANGE AND GROWTH MINDSET

Just as teachers felt ill-prepared for virtual learning (Ireri, 2021), principals were equally as unprepared (Hayes, Flowers, & Williams, 2021). However, both groups of professionals also shared another similarity: they had to adopt a growth mindset. A growth mindset indicates individuals who take challenges as opportunities to learn and improve (Dweck, 2006). Jack, a first-year principal, stated,

> I don't know what could have prepared me for this role because it kinda neutralized everybody. You know, whether you've been in education twenty years or in education for one year, we were all learning on the same level. [The pandemic] leveled the playing field.

Most educators were in the same boat, and the need for change was pressing and urgent with the abrupt shut down of schools. Donna, a high school principal with three years of experience, stated, "During times like these, you have to be prepared to make changes, even if it's the morning of. You have to be prepared to do that." So that is what educators did. Was the transition perfect? Absolutely not. Were mistakes made? Absolutely yes. However, mistakes provide more opportunities to learn, and this should be communicated as a part of the improvement process in order to impact organizational practices (Weinzimmer & Esken, 2017).

Administrators, just like teachers, should not fear failure. Hanna, an experienced high school principal, stated,

> Just like we have to support our teachers and we were there for them, we have to say it's okay to fail. It's okay to try something. And if it doesn't work, it's okay. As a principal, you don't know how many teachers came and sat across the desk from me and just cried. And I had to take that all in for them . . . and try to find solutions for their problems.

Administrators had to do the same and rely on one another to solve the problems they were facing. Because most were engaged in a novel experience, no one person was considered the expert, and all could learn from one another.

The challenge is to capitalize on this mindset. Continue to learn, grow, and be fearful of returning to the status quo. As the dust clears, make sure to continue the conversations about curricular and assessment improvements as well as integrating technology. Jack, a first-year principal, stated,

> The advice I'd give to other principals is to reach out to other principals, trust the data, figure out how to disseminate it, and use that to drive your instruction and your leadership teams. You don't have to be the expert. You don't have to have all the answers, but figure it out, learn, and just put yourself in a position to make sure you're successful and your schools are successful.

Remember, with the use of video conferencing, this can be made more accessible than one once thought.

In the *Principal's Corner* below, the importance of sustaining the successful systems created during the pandemic are addressed. Remember the lessons learned from the pandemic and continue the positive practices while making them systemic. Learn from the mistakes made and continue to support teachers with educational and emotional needs. Who knows what the next year will bring!

> *Jim Rohn said, "If you are not willing to risk the usual, you will have to settle for the ordinary." One thing we can say at Warrior Nation is that we do not settle for ordinary or mediocrity. The successes I love to see are our students growing, advocating, and articulating for themselves and others. Seeing our students grow and become first-generation graduates from their families and go on to a four-year, two-year, or even the military to fulfill their dreams for their next journey in life. Success is not only turning a school around but sustaining the systems created for teachers, the community, and especially our students to grow beyond their expectations. They see the potential and execute the plan despite the obstacles and challenges they overcome, perseverance.*
>
> *"People who succeed have momentum. The more they succeed, the more they want to succeed, and the more they find a way to succeed. Similarly, when someone is failing, the tendency is to get on a downward spiral that can even become a self-fulfilling prophecy," says Tony Robbins. At Warrior Nation, we find the correct ways to succeed for our community but especially for our students. It is the Warrior Way.*

SUMMARY

During the Covid-19 pandemic, school leaders faced many challenges to include the need for more social/emotional support of staff and students. This additional need underscored the anxiety levels felt by all, not just about the educational process and the necessary changes, but also the fears for health and safety.

School leaders were also challenged with self-care during this time. The school-based problems and need for constant communication also took a toll on principals' personal well-being.

Additional challenges most assuredly rested with the lack of student engagement and anticipated achievement levels. All across the world, reports of learning losses have been described. Leaders had to find a way to battle the losses to come. Technology also provided a challenge for many: The ascertainment of technology, the training, and the use of technology provided many obstacles to overcome.

Successes during the pandemic, however, should not be ignored. Foremost among them was the development of a growth mindset, particularly among those leaders who may have been described as stagnant in the traditional setting. Because of this growth mindset, some of the challenges became successes.

Social/emotional support of staff flourished during this time, and team cohesion is reported as stronger than ever. In addition, technology proficiencies have blossomed, and plans are being made for future uses.

POLISHING THE DIAMOND

1. What are three challenges faced by school leaders during the pandemic?
2. How did school leaders overcome those challenges?
3. What are three successes experienced during the pandemic?
4. How can the lessons learned transfer to the traditional setting?

REFERENCES

Almeida, D., Davis, K., Lee, S., Lawson, K., Walter, K., & Moen, P. (2016). Supervisor support buffers daily psychological and physiological reactivity to work-to-family conflict. *Journal of Marriage and Family, 78*(1), 165–179.

Anderson, E., Hayes, S., & Carpenter, B. (2020). Principal as caregiver of all: Responding to needs of others and self. CPRE Policy Briefs. Accessed https://repository.upenn.edu/cpre_policybriefs/92

Berkovich, I., & Eyal, O. (2018). Principals' emotional support and teachers' emotional reframing: The mediating role of principals' supportive communication strategies. *Psychology in the Schools, 55*(7), 867–879.

Day, C. (2013). Teacher quality in the twenty first century: New lives, old truths. In X. D. Zhu & K. M. Zeichner (eds.), *Preparing teachers for the 21st century* (pp. 21–38). Heidelberg, Germany: Springer.

Dorn, E., Hancock, B., Sarakatsannis, J., & Viruleg, E. (2020). COVID-19 and student learning in the United States: The hurt could last a lifetime. Retrieved from https://www.apucis.com/frontend-assets/porto/initial-reports/COVID-19-and-student-learning-in-the-United-States-FINAL.pdf.pagespeed.ce.VHbS948yF4.pdf

Dweck, C. (2006). *Mindset: The psychology of success*. New York: Ballentine Books.

Hayes, S. D., Flowers, J., & Williams, S. M. (2021, January). Constant communication: Rural principals' leadership practices during a global pandemic. *Frontiers in Education, 5,* 277.

Ireri, M. (2021). Teachers'' and parents' preparedness to support virtual learning during the Covid-19 pandemic in Kenya. *African Journal of Empirical Research, 2*(1), 95–101.

Jan, H. (2017). Teacher of 21st century: Characteristics and development. *Research on Humanities and Social Sciences*, 7(9), 50–54.

Kaul, M., VanGronigen, B. A., & Simon, N. S. (2020). Calm during crisis: School principal approaches to crisis management during the COVID-19 pandemic. CPRE Policy Briefs. Retrieved from https://repository.upenn.edu/cpre_policybriefs/89

Kuhfeld, M., Soland, J., Tarasawa, B., Johnson, A., Ruzek, E., & Liu, J. (2020). Projecting the potential impact of COVID-19 school closures on academic achievement. *Educational Researcher*, 49(8), 549–565.

Kuhfeld, M., & Tarasawa, B. (2020). The COVID-19 slide: What summer learning loss can tell us about the potential impact of school closures on student academic achievement. NWEA. Accessed https://www.nwea.org/content/uploads/2020/05/Collaborative-Brief_Covid19-Slide-APR20.pdf

Rasheed, R. A., Kamsin, A., Abdullah, N. A., Kakudi, H. A., Ali, A. S., Musa, A. S., & Yahaya, A. S. (2020). Self-regulated learning in flipped classrooms: A systematic literature review. *International Journal of Information and Education Technology*, 10(11), 848–853.

Saad, N., & Sankaran, S. (2020). Technology proficiency in teaching and facilitating. In *Oxford Research Encyclopedia of Education*. Oxford: Oxford University Press.

Somech, A. (2016). The cost of going the extra mile: The relationship between teachers' organizational citizenship behavior, role stressors, and strain with the buffering effect of job autonomy. *Teachers and Teaching*, 22(4), 426–447.

Torres Martín, C., Acal, C., El Honrani, M., & Mingorance Estrada, Á. C. (2021). Impact on the virtual learning environment due to COVID-19. *Sustainability*, 13(2), 582.

Weinzimmer, L. G., & Esken, C. A. (2017). Learning from mistakes: How mistake tolerance positively affects organizational learning and performance. *The Journal of Applied Behavioral Science*, 53(3), 322–348.

Yue, C., Men, L., Ferguson, M. (2021). Examining the effects of internal communication and emotional culture on employees' organizational identification. *International Journal of Business Communication*, 58(2), 169–195.

Conclusion

During the Covid-19 pandemic, school leaders across the world were faced with new challenges. Once schools were shut down amid the "stay at home" orders given by state and local governments, principals encountered an abrupt transition to virtual leadership. Teachers struggled to provide seamless instruction, and students struggled to remain engaged in the learning process. Of course, these were just a few of the difficulties experienced by school leaders.

A mixed-method study of South Carolina principals and superintendents highlighted the challenges and successes experienced by all during this trying time. The lessons learned should not be isolated to the pandemic but should be transferred to traditional school settings. Though schools plan to fully return to face-to-face instruction in the near future, virtual elements of schooling will not disappear. In addition, the lessons learned also highlight best practices that are beneficial to all principals in the brick-and-mortar setting. They simply will serve to strengthen leadership skills universally.

District leaders should also heed the lessons learned in providing support for principals and professional development in areas that may not have been previously imagined. The impact of the principalship during the pandemic may have ramifications of further leadership shortages if leaders are not prepared for what the future brings.

The study conducted during the pandemic revealed four themes, so the comparison to the four characteristics of a diamond was utilized throughout the book: carat, color, clarity, and cut. This classification system was used because the gem of an effective virtual principal was found amid the study. The practices she employed benefited her students, staff, and community. Districts should all work to polish the gem that is the virtual principal for the sake of all.

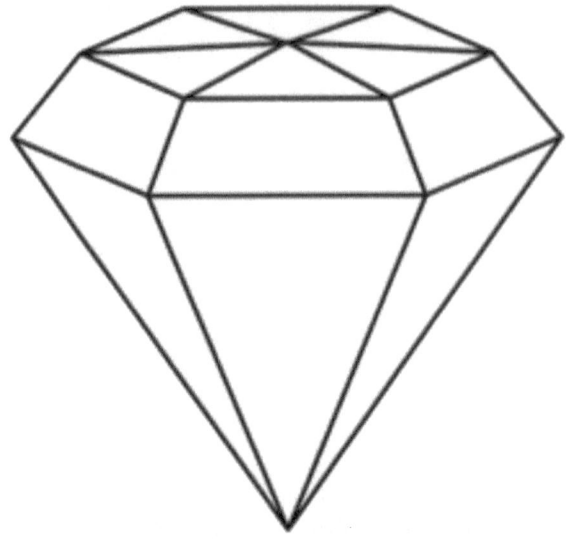

Carat	Color	Clarity	Cut
The carat is the weight of the diamond—the weight of the impact of Covid-19 on principals—confidence and growth.	The visible color of the stone can be compared to the visible factors in the principalship—communication, soft skills, etc.	The clearer, the more brilliant the stone—the more value. Instructional leadership and systems approaches make expectations clear.	The cut of the stone is determined by its depth and angles. These factors affect how light shines through the stone. Examining successes and challenges is akin to the cut.

About the Authors

Dr. Lee Westberry has over twenty years' experience as a school administrator at the middle school, high school, and district levels. Prior to serving as administrator, she was an English teacher. Most recently, Dr. Westberry has served as an Assistant Professor of Educational Leadership, Director of Program Development and Enhancement, and Program Coordinator in the Zucker Family School of Education at The Citadel in Charleston, South Carolina. Dr. Westberry also serves as a visiting professor for Clemson University in the doctoral program.

Dr. Westberry continues to support principal leaders in the state through professional development offerings and consulting through her consulting firm FLIP Educational Group. Dr. Westberry has previously published two books in that vein: *Putting the Pieces Together: A Systems Approach to School Leadership* and *The Final Piece: A Systems Approach to School Leadership*.

In addition to her passion for education, Dr. Westberry also has a passion for her family. Married for thirty years this year to her high school sweetheart, Dr. Westberry strives to be the best wife to Danny and mother to her two daughters, Warner and Sophie.

Dr. Tara Hornor currently serves as an Associate Professor and Coordinator of Higher Education Leadership Programs in the Zucker Family School of Education with a joint appointment to The Citadel's Department of Leadership Studies. She has over twenty years of higher education leadership experience, previously serving as Associate Provost for Planning, Assessment, and Evaluation and Dean of Enrollment Management at The Citadel, providing leadership for the institution's strategic planning, accreditation, assessment, institutional research, admissions, financial aid, and graduate college offices. Dr. Hornor holds a Ph.D. in Higher Education Administration from the University of Arizona and master's degrees in school counseling, instructional design, and human resource management. She is also a 2014 graduate of Harvard University's Institute for Management and Leadership in Education (MLE) and a 2009 graduate of Harvard University's Performance Assessment in Higher Education Institute.

Mona Lise Dickson was going to be an actuary, but God had a different plan for her. After leaving Florida and residing in Beaufort, South Carolina, she taught mathematics at Beaufort High School and coached girls' varsity basketball for fourteen years. She continued with thirteen years of experience as a school administrator in both middle and high schools and is affectionately known as the Olivia Pope of school principals. Recently, Ms. Dickson was promoted to the Executive Director of School Transformation in Beaufort County School District and is pursuing her doctorate in Education Improvement Science.

Mona Lise Dickson is not only dedicated to transforming schools but to her family. Ms. Dickson is married to Charles Dickson, and together they have four children: Racquel, Haley, Caisey, and Michael. In addition, they have four grandchildren: Sydney, Skylar, Dominic, and Alaia.